ADVANCE PRAISE FOR

Building Connections

"*Building Connections: Spiritual Dimensions of Teaching* is well written and touches upon the connection of teaching to one's personal journey. It wonderfully reviews the importance of reflection and describes how reflection on culture and self is central to excellence in teaching. Eileen M. Cunningham shares her own story and powerfully leads the reader to understand this central aspect of teaching. She easily shows reflection is key to teaching and, even more profoundly, to fully understanding the spirituality that is part of every teacher's day. This book is a must read for those who prepare teachers and for those who want to develop fully into excellent teachers."

Ronald R. Cromwell, Dean, School of Education and Allied Studies,
Bridgewater State College, Massachusetts

"This book addresses the spiritual journey of teachers, whether they are entering the classroom for the first time or they have been in the profession for many years. Since, however, their spiritual lives are inextricably bound to their teaching careers, it is the vast complex of relations that constitute their instruction that is the subject of reflection...."

Eileen Clifford, O.P., Associate Vicar for Education,
Archdiocese of New York

"The author, through her personal, professional, and faith experiences, clearly envisions and activates teaching to that of a ministry. The notion of teaching being a spiritual dimension goes beyond simple reflection in practice and is reminiscent of the observed behavior of expert teachers looking at the affective impact and 'rightness' of their instruction. A must read for those charged with the preservice preparation of teachers for our elementary, middle, and secondary schools; for those responsible for and participating in continuing professional development, this book offers a multiplicity of thought-provoking gems that could well serve as foci of reflective exercises and activities in enriching the capacity of all teachers to ensure all students learn to their potential."

Charles C. Mackey, Jr., Executive Coordinator,
New York State Education Department

Building Connections

Studies in the Postmodern Theory of Education

Joe L. Kincheloe and Shirley R. Steinberg
General Editors

Vol. 130

PETER LANG
New York • Washington, D.C./Baltimore • Bern
Frankfurt am Main • Berlin • Brussels • Vienna • Oxford

Eileen M. Cunningham, O.P.

Building Connections

Spiritual Dimensions of Teaching

PETER LANG
New York • Washington, D.C./Baltimore • Bern
Frankfurt am Main • Berlin • Brussels • Vienna • Oxford

Library of Congress Cataloging-in-Publication Data
Cunningham, Eileen M.
Building connections: spiritual dimensions
of teaching / Eileen M. Cunningham, O.P.
p. cm. — (Counterpoints; vol. 130)
Includes bibliographical references (p.   ) and index.
1. Teaching—Religious aspects. 2. Multicultural education. 3. Critical
pedagogy. I. Title. II. Counterpoints (New York, N.Y.); v. 130.
LB1027.2 .C85   371.102—dc21   99-052778
ISBN 0-8204-4860-5
ISSN 1058-1634

Die Deutsche Bibliothek-CIP-Einheitsaufnahme
Cunningham, Eileen M.:
Building connections: spiritual dimensions
of teaching / Eileen M. Cunningham, O.P.
−New York; Washington, D.C./Baltimore; Bern;
Frankfurt am Main; Berlin; Brussels; Vienna; Oxford: Lang.
(Counterpoints; Vol. 130)
ISBN 0-8204-4860-5

Cover design by Lisa Dillon
Cover photo "Hands Across America" by Eileen M. Cunningham, O.P.

The paper in this book meets the guidelines for permanence and durability
of the Committee on Production Guidelines for Book Longevity
of the Council of Library Resources.

© 2001 Peter Lang Publishing, Inc., New York

All rights reserved.
Reprint or reproduction, even partially, in all forms such as microfilm,
xerography, microfiche, microcard, and offset strictly prohibited.

Printed in the United States of America

In memory of my parents
Paddy and Jo Callaghan Cunningham
whose devotion, faithfulness, and commitment
taught me many valuable lessons;
and of my brother Pat
who encouraged me to finish writing this book,
even during our last conversation.

Table of Contents

Foreword ix

Preface xi

Acknowledgments xiii

Introduction 1

Chapter One
Building Connections 9

Chapter Two
Spirituality 23

Chapter Three
Personal Influences of a Spiritual Nature 35

Chapter Four
Cultural Autobiography 45

Chapter Five
Stereotypes 59

Chapter Six
Analyzing Assumptions 65

Chapter Seven
Social Analysis 75

Chapter Eight
Culturally Responsive Pedagogy 85

Chapter Nine
Envisioning the Future 103

Chapter Ten
Effective Teachers 109

Epilogue 117

References 119

Index 121

Foreword

Eileen Cunningham invites her readers to take a journey, a journey that is fraught with new and unfamiliar encounters—some frightening, some inspiring, but all transformative. As I read this volume I find myself accompanying Eileen in her travels and then find that I have at some point shifted to my own experiences and I am meandering down my own path of life, trying to figure out who I am and how I came to be the way I am. This is exactly Cunningham's intent as she leads us through her own life's encounters. She invites each of us to take a similar journey, examining who we are in time and space so that we can come to an acceptance of self and ultimately an openness to others.

The first chapters introduce us to her travels to Pakistan and Peru, and her encounters with different faces of poverty and spirituality. Her reactions to these experiences cause her to ask herself who she is and how her own life has led to a pattern of beliefs and behavior. She comes to understand how her frustration and fear at the unfamiliar are symbols of ways she is held captive by her own experiences. We share one of her great awakenings as she tries to cope and, looking around, forces herself to realize that she is surrounded by people who are engaged in all the normal business of quite ordinary lives. Soon we see a much more confident Cunningham, wearing native garb and sitting on the floor eating local food. While the dress, food, and customs do not define the essence of a group of people, sharing such manifestations of a culture allows the visitor to slip inside indigenous skin and share an experience more closely.

The next journey is an intensely personal one in which she explores her spiritual and cultural self through autobiography. We see a young girl from an Irish immigrant family in the Bronx living in the midst of other immigrant families as she encounters similarities and differences in the people around her. She tells a story of an uncle's remark about a black person that became an important force in shaping her perception of racial differences. While the remark could be considered patronizing and stereotypical, Cunningham is as accepting of her own cultural background as she is of the background of others. Rather than be defensive about the remark, she accepts it as being helpful to her in avoiding fear of people whose skin is a different color. She also acknowledges that it taught her that seemingly positive comments can also be derogatory stereotypes.

Cunningham's next journey is into classrooms—whether they be classrooms of children or classrooms of adults preparing to be teachers. Here each of the previous journeys becomes a metaphor for understanding the process by which a teacher comes to understand the lives of the students. In each of these new territories Cunningham shows us how openness to the experience and viewpoints of others enables the teacher to build the respect, sensitivity, and acceptance necessary to culturally responsive teaching. In the final chapters we see how fear and suspicion inhibit teaching and learning. She gives us powerful examples of fear paralyzing students and leads us into a rarer glimpse of fear shaping teacher's actions. In learning to step confidently into the cultures of others and into the culture group she grew up in, Cunningham gives us a model of a teacher learning to step equally confidently into the classroom that will become the nexus for the culture of the students, the culture of the teacher, and the culture of the larger community in which the school exists.

Today more and more people are intentionally choosing to teach—not simply becoming a teacher because it is a vocation accessible to them. With this intention often comes a strong sense of mission, founded in spiritual commitment or a sense of service, whether or not the teachers are part of an organized religion. *Building Connections* puts this spirituality into a context that enables novice teachers and those who teach them to begin the personal journey. This is one of the few books that really helps us see that culturally responsive teaching must begin in the hearts and minds of teachers, teachers who have come to accept themselves and their own culture and who are open to the identities and cultural expressions of others.

Carol Merz, Dean
School of Education
University of Puget Sound

Preface

In this book I explore some of the practices cultivated by men and women who are dedicated professional teachers. These practices are not identified as criteria for certification, nor are they listed among content standards. Literature and research that are focused on the professional development of teachers come closest to naming them within the paradigm of reflective practice. Indeed, reflection is a starting point, but it is through the unique lens of a spirituality of teaching that the practice of reflection is pursued in this book. Its major premise is that teachers who engage in honest reflection, by examining the contexts and situations of their professional practice, discover spiritual dimensions of teaching and cultivate a spirituality that enlivens their enthusiasm and competence for the challenges they encounter regularly. These challenges are encountered in classrooms, schools, and neighborhoods on which converge our culturally diverse population for the purpose of teaching and learning.

The process of education is changed with each new generation of youngsters born in the United States of America and with each new wave of immigrants to its shores. Those who teach in this culturally diverse society are well aware of its complexity. The challenges of cultural diversity, society's perceptions, expectations and accompanying criticism, changing patterns of life in general, access to decent housing, nutrition, and equitable medical services are all variables that compound the challenges faced by teachers on a daily basis. For the most part, they are met successfully and effectively, but there's always room for improvement.

Experienced teachers call on an inner strength to sustain their efforts to meet these challenges. Novice teachers soon learn that they need support and encouragement to pursue their mission to teach. I suggest that the act of contemplating the contexts and situations of their lives is a vibrant and essential factor in the lives of those teachers, who acknowledge their need for an interior force that will help them in ways that may surprise and delight.

At this historical turn-of-the-century moment, every aspect of education (including methodology and materials, student achievement and international rankings, funding sources and salaries, values, length of the school year and school governance) is challenged. Politically driven decisions are frequently divorced from the realities of classroom instruction and the real needs of learners. These external forces can interfere with teachers' efforts to be effective educators. Yet, teachers are held accountable, and in the process their sense of efficacy, of being in a position to influence their profession, is undermined. Teachers need to be affirmed in their professional knowledge and practices and to be confident in their ability to connect with culturally and linguistically diverse learners and their parents. Teachers need to acknowledge their shortcomings, accept responsibility for those aspects of their profession that need changing and that they can change, and be ready to make these changes.

Eileen M. Cunningham, O.P.

Acknowledgments

From the beginning of this project to its end, I have felt the support of my community, family, colleagues, and friends. Many members of my Dominican community supported me in various ways. Marie Jean Dempsey, O.P., Catherine Moran, O.P., and Patricia Ann Reilly, O.P. read the manuscript in its various stages, suggested revisions, and offered unfailing encouragement. Artist Adele Myers, O.P. guided the design of the cover. Members of my community in Pakistan welcomed me and shared their life, education, and traditions with me. They introduced me to a totally new culture in gentle yet eye-opening ways. In Peru, my dearest friend, Maureen also introduced me to an entirely different culture. In Peru, as in Pakistan, I was welcomed into the homes of so many people and have developed friends for life.

Many of my cousins in Ireland and Scotland welcomed me into their homes and provided places where I could combine family visits with writing. At home, Tricia and Tom Mullane let me use their home in Montauk, N.Y., where I did so much of the writing and editing of this manuscript.

My students' openness and honesty never fail to impress me. They continue to teach me about the complexity of working effectively with the culturally diverse student population.

At all times, and regardless of the simplicity or magnitude of my questions, members of the Peter Lang staff were pleasant, helpful, and prompt in responding. My gratitude to Jacqueline Pavolvic, Jean Achard, Sophie Appel, and Chris Myers. Series editor Shirley Steinberg's immediate and enthusiastic response to my prospectus helped me believe in the worth of this project.

I treasure the encouragement and friendship of Jacqueline Jordan Irvine of Emory University, Carol Merz of the University of Puget Sound, Ron Cromwell of Bridgewater State University, Charles Mackey of the New York State Department of Education, and Eileen Clifford, O.P. of the Archdiocese of New York. In unique ways, each one has contributed to this book. My colleagues at St. Thomas Aquinas College have been unwavering in their support and confidence of my work. Special thanks to Fred Sambor, F.M.S., and Pearl Solomon whose superb ability to use the computer helped me to format the manuscript.

Last but not least, I want to thank my sister Joanne and my brother Tom just for being who they are. I am sure that their memories of some of the events I describe differ from mine. Our perceptions of events will necessarily differ because of the experience each of us brings to the contexts and situations of our lives. Thus, I look forward to some lively discussions.

Introduction

There's a mystique to writing a book. The task seems, at first glance and when taken as a whole, to be beyond accomplishment. Indeed, when I think about undertaking a task of this magnitude, the thoughts are daunting. This is especially true because in this book I proclaim my own truth, thereby accepting complete and profound responsibility for its content. Who am I to assume such trust or even to think that others might be interested in reading what I have to say? There is no specific answer to this question except to say that I do so to articulate to a broad audience some understandings that have evolved as a result of personal experiences with cultural diversity. Included in these experiences are extensive travels to foreign countries, visits to many schools and teaching experiences in a few, and meetings with teachers and students who taught me how education is pursued in their culture. Living among native people gave me a glimpse of their lives as few tourists see it. Moreover, I was raised in a large immigrant family with close ties to home. A first-generation American, my roots are in Ireland. I grew up in New York City, in the Bronx, and I frequently return to my own native land.

The ideas developed throughout the book also come from my professional experiences over the past thirty-six years. These include teaching on the elementary and college levels, listening to teachers share their experiences, participating in conferences, serving on boards of Catholic high schools and a public day care center, and working with teachers in the inner city and in the suburbs.

What I gleaned from these experiences had an impact on both the personal and professional lives of the teachers with whom I shared my insights. They told me that their personal and professional identities were enhanced through such sharing. They encouraged me to write this book. These colleagues challenged my statements and helped me to see the ramifications of my ideas with greater clarity. They helped me realize that the thoughts I share are pertinent for all teachers whether they work in the inner city or in the suburbs because diversity pervades the population.

Basically, the book calls on teachers to adopt a thoughtful stance. It encourages them to reflect on their encounters with students and their parents, with their peers and their supervisors. The process of reflection is well within the reach of all teachers but it may not be within their present mind-set. If some teachers find my ideas to be similar to their own practices, let them be affirmed in how they pursue their profession. Let those who find the ideas to be novel test them for potential application in their professional arenas.

Through the practice of thoughtful reflection teachers can develop a greater degree of confidence as they pursue their calling or their mission to teach. Reflecting or pondering ideas and interactions at depth can lead to deeper self-knowledge in relation to others. This in turn can transform interpersonal encounters and broaden teachers' vision. Reflection empowers teachers to consider from a fresh perspective the multifaceted ramifications of building connections with culturally diverse peoples, whether they are learners, parents, or colleagues. Reflection moves teachers to become critical analyzers of the contexts, situations, and expectations that surround education. Reflection enlivens teachers' spirits and supports them as they pursue their vocation. The potential to influence even those who challenge the effectiveness of ideas frequently creates new understandings. Don't be put off if the contents don't find a home in you.

Who Should Read This Book?

Teachers whose professional practice is carried out in a context of cultural diversity should read this book. So too should teachers who want to enjoy more than satisfactory interpersonal relationships with students and their families, and with colleagues. Many of these teachers recognize the need to examine interactions and to change attitudes or behaviors that interfere with interpersonal relationships. Many of these teachers want to touch the human spirit of their students and acknowledge what is decent. They value goodness, truth, beauty, and justice, those intangibles that comprise what

Maslow (1968) refers to as the higher needs of humans. Teachers who work to create effective learning environments also celebrate virtues of courtesy, openness, honesty, civility, and magnanimity. The book is written for teachers who want to imagine a future for what it can be, for teachers who want to participate in change and who know that change starts with themselves and spreads slowly to those in their immediate environment.

This book is written for teachers and other school people to stimulate their thoughts about ways to build connections with culturally diverse learners and their parents, peers, and supervisors. Diversity incorporates such variations as ethnicity, gender, race, religion, sexual orientation, heritage language, country of origin, and socioeconomic background. Within these categories are sheltered a myriad of other variations. There is a tendency to fear the breadth of diversity and to persuade ourselves that values such as democracy, equality, and freedom flourish only when everyone and everything acts out of the same perspective. Such fear is irrational and opposes the very principles of these values. In contrast, I suggest that diversity isn't necessarily divisive. What is divisive is what we make of it. Do we fear it or celebrate it? Do we acknowledge and respect it or deny and denigrate it? Do we use it to help us understand multiple perspectives or to validate our personal perspective? Diversity is a reality. It is both a descriptor and a revelation. It gives us a glimpse of the Creator, whose all-encompassing wisdom contains and loves the beauty that is inherent in diversity.

My Hopes

This book is written in joyful remembrance of my own journey, despite the difficulties I encountered along the way. By sharing the awareness that evolve from personal experiences with people of diverse cultures, I hope to encourage teachers to encounter in a critically reflective way their own reality with diverse students. The reality of teachers resides with learners and their families, in schools, classrooms, and local communities, with colleagues and supervisors. These form a collective group, assembled for the purpose of teaching the next generation of adults, leaders and members of our society. The collective consciousness of this group must endorse the idea that what people do today does indeed make a difference in tomorrow's world.

This book is written with sensitivity to those dedicated persons who have responded to an inner voice that tells them to be concerned about youth and about the future of the human race. The more I hear prospective teachers explain why they want to pursue this career of service, the more convinced I am that they actually describe a *mission*.

Hope for the Mission of Teachers
The term mission is used frequently in the United States. We've sent astronauts on missions to outer space and humanitarians on missions to many of the countries around the world to help these countries in their efforts toward freedom or democracy or relief from some inhuman suffering.

Teachers are sent into classrooms with less fanfare and perhaps with a bit more of a critical eye on the outcomes of their mission. Society in general can disregard the missions to outer space and to other countries. These don't touch lives as personally as does education. Most adults have attended school and currently support education through taxes. They feel free to critique it, primarily by linking teachers' competence to students' performance on standardized tests. Yet, these represent merely a fraction of the reality of the mission of teaching in such a diverse society.

This book is primarily written to inspire teachers, to encourage them in their mission to teach the youth of this country, and to influence its future. Teaching is a very demanding profession. Because schools are institutions that provide for children's needs, teachers are frequently expected to make up for what is lacking in the society at large or in families or both. Consequently, schools are considered places where children can be safe, where they can socialize, be taught manners and values, and where they can be given breakfast and lunch. In addition, schools must also help children achieve academically to a standard that will place the United States on a par with other world powers. When these expectations are not met, the teachers are generally blamed.

Little acknowledgment is given to these diverse expectations that society places on schools and teachers. We rarely hear that these expectations detract from the actual mission of the schools and of the teachers. In spite of this, most teachers strive to be effective promoters of learning, to connect authentically to students and reverence their human dignity, while teaching youngsters what they need to know in order to live decent lives.

Teachers who critically analyze the impact of society's expectations on their mission (Giroux, 1994) can address what challenges or undermines it. This sounds like a highly charged suggestion that many teachers prefer to avoid because they feel it diverts attention from the students' learning and their own mission. However, I believe that the knowledge that comes from such an analysis can help teachers pursue their mission more effectively. To do so, they need a steady and reliable source of renewing energy to sustain them and an objective set of criteria against which to measure their decisions. Whether they know it or not, all teachers have an interior spring, a source of renewing energy that motivates and supports them. Surprisingly, only a small percentage of teachers dip into it, and those who do discover its promise return to it regularly. Others need encouragement and know-how in order to do so. This book is written to provide such encouragement and know-how and to suggest ways that teachers can connect with their interior source while effectively connecting with learners. They can do this within a personal spirituality of teaching that transforms them and their mission.

Hope for the Spirituality of Teachers
The term *spirituality* is used here to name the way people view their daily lives and make sense of its practicalities and jumbles, its hopes and dreams (Woods, 1998). Teachers who attempt to do this will find the journey both intimidating and enlightening; intimidating in that what becomes known may seem at first glance to be overwhelming; enlightening in that what is revealed may help them tap more deeply into the reservoir of their spirituality. If this book encourages those who read it to nurture their spirituality, to claim their values, and to carry out their mission with confidence in their potential to create a just society, its writing will have been worthwhile.

I propose that teachers use readily available documents and theories as the lens through which to pursue their spirituality. The International Declaration of Human Rights, promulgated in 1943 by the United Nations, the hierarchy of human needs as presented by Maslow (1968), and the stages in the development of a multicultural perspective as developed by Wurzel (1988) form a framework through which teachers can reflect on the pertinent issues and decisions related to their mission of teaching. The choice of these sources is deliberate. They are known by teachers, or are easily accessible. They are clearly articulated and reveal the complexity of education. They encourage deep probing of school-related issues and incidents through generic descriptors of needs, rights, or conditions that are not context-bound but rather focused on persons. Generic criteria are free of the variables that might otherwise cloud thought processes and affect just decisions. These include ethnicity, gender, race, religion, sexual orientation, heritage language, country of origin, and socioeconomic background. The ideal condition does not negate these variables. Rather, it lays them aside so as to focus primarily on the inherent human dignity and the worthiness of students, parents, and colleagues.

I have benefited greatly from my personal pursuit of a *spirituality of teaching*. It has enhanced my understanding of the diverse society of our country as well as my efforts to connect with people. The benefits I have derived inspire me to make them available to others.

The Contents of the Book

I develop the theme of building connections between and among people in Chapter One. Through thoughtful and honest reflection on encounters, these connections become strengthened. Such reflection requires a personal perspective marked by respect for the dignity of the individual, hope in the human desire to live a good life, perseverance to withhold judgment and remain in suspended animation until issues are settled, and sufficient self-confidence to pursue the desired outcome. The task of building connections leads a person from an ethnocentric perspective to a multicultural outlook, one that inspires a life lived in peace and harmony. Yet, achieving peace and harmony takes time and effort. It requires interactive contact and dialogue and adjustments.

Spirituality, currently a topic of great interest, is explored in Chapter Two. This topic is examined from the perspective of the spiritual dimensions of teaching. Perhaps the most obvious question to be asked is whether such an entity exists. If so, what evidence do we have of it? How is it expressed? How does it motivate? How can it be fostered? The idea of writing about spirituality suggested itself as I reflected on the nature of the interactions and the atmosphere that generally prevails when teachers encounter significant issues in a thoughtful and reflective manner. The mysterious nature of spirituality is apparent during such times. It surprises and delights those who have searched for answers to many of life's deepest questions.

In Chapter Three I attempt to unite the themes of building connections and spirituality to represent the spiritual dimensions of teaching. In so doing, I share personal influences that have guided my rationale for developing the format for my work with teachers. Readers will notice that the rationale and format stem from my own reliance on the process of reflection that I encourage all teachers to learn and practice. Included in this chapter is a discussion of how teachers respond to the ideas of building connections and to the spiritual dimensions of teaching.

Additional reflections on the factors that have influenced my world view are presented in Chapter Four, in the form of a cultural autobiography. Childhood experiences, professional assignments, travel, and life among people whose language and customs differ significantly from my own weave a global perspective, a lens through which I view the world and monitor my outlook. Teachers who research their own cultural autobiography create their own lens, with an inner eye focused on their attitudes and responses to cultural diversity and with a global eye toward the connections they build with other school people.

Chapters Five through Eight examine and explain applications of reflection that awaken the awareness and knowledge of teachers. Chapter Five addresses the topic of stereotypes and presents a format for using reflection to uncover them and to confront their implications. Teachers who have been introduced to this technique discover the difference between stereotypes that are negative and thus harmful and generalizations that are descriptive of the members of a group. However, during this exercise, teachers experience a significant level of discomfort. This is a natural reaction to sensitive topics, ones we generally avoid talking about.

Chapter Six introduces a process that guides the analysis of assumptions. This format for reflection helps people to probe their motivations and clarify the expectations they bring to contexts and situations. We all have expectations but we may not always aware of them. Sometimes we hold unrealistic expectations for others. Sometimes we ascribe motivations to others out of our own unspecified expectations. The process I describe is just as revealing but less threatening than the stereotyping exercise discussed in the previous chapter. Teachers generally agree that it helps them to clarify their thinking and ultimately to state their expectations more effectively. In Chapter Seven another application of critical reflection, namely, a social analysis of the Hansel and Gretel story, is presented. This reflection prompts teachers to think more broadly about the lives of learners, their families, and their neighborhoods. Such an analysis can lead teachers to in-depth interaction with the variables of the lives of students. It can help teachers think about the children who sometimes bring to school more needs and responsibilities than we might imagine.

The next two chapters describe specific actions that teachers can take in response to the knowledge and awareness that emerge from the various applications of reflection. These subsequent actions allow teachers to put their spirituality to the test, to let its benefits show forth in the decisions they make on a daily basis and in the hope they have for building connections to the future.

Chapter Eight focuses on what teachers do best. They teach. They make choices about pedagogy and materials and formats and assignments. It is my hope that teachers who pursue their own spirituality of teaching will make choices that respect the multicultural perspective that they are developing. I suggest that culturally responsive pedagogy is a valid choice for these teachers. This pedagogy enhances the capabilities of learners. It validates their family traditions and heritage language by building them into the ideas, skills, and dispositions to be learned. Effective teaching demands skillful pedagogy, credible content knowledge, and well-developed interpersonal skills. Successful learning occurs in a learning community. Culturally responsive pedagogy can help teachers and learners achieve these ideals.

In Chapter Nine I discuss a process that can enliven hope in the future. It is called envisioning the future and it engages teachers in the processes of dreaming and creating. The future I envision is one without violence or at least one in which violence is quelled. I suggest that alternative responses to violence can be found by channeling energies toward creative works that invite others to share in the sorrow or fear that might otherwise erupt in destructive forms.

In Chapter Ten I present a vision of an ideal teacher. This vision has emerged from interviews with persons in pre-service teacher preparation programs. In addition, I include reflections and other examples of the way teachers have responded to the various perspectives presented throughout the text. I believe that including the products of teachers helps to clarify and validate what I have written. It also helps me to appreciate the magnificent nature of a mission that is revealed through the reflective writings of teachers. How these teachers have responded to these ideas is a measure of their efforts to connect with the students in their charge. As always, I continue to learn from these teachers who are my students as well as my teachers.

My final thoughts of inspiration are presented in a brief Epilogue.

Chapter One
Building Connections

> *In this first chapter I set forth an idea about effective, respectful, and reverent connections with people in schools and classrooms. These people include teachers, learners, parents, and neighborhood business personnel. Very often the imagery used to describe connections alludes to a gap that needs to be bridged. Such imagery implies that something is lacking or needs to be fixed. I would encourage a different vision, one of connecting one human to another on an equal, horizontal plane in a spirit of reciprocity and humility. Such a spirit celebrates the positive influence that diversity has on society. Diversity is the visible expression of our common humanity. It is a reflection of our Creator.*

Imagine the Grand Canyon, a huge abyss that attracts tourists to the southwestern part of the United States from all over the world. Its magnitude encompasses vestiges of life layered in its rocks century after century, change upon change. Imagine the reactions of those people who first discovered this phenomenon of nature. What did they think? How did they react? Did they shrink back in fear? Did they approach it with boldness or curiosity? Did they let its resources nourish and sustain them? Were they challenged by its breadth? Did they ever think it an aberration and attempt to fill it up?

Records of its discovery, no doubt, reveal some of the impressions and thoughts of those early people. And I am certain that many of those who ventured to conquer this natural wonder soon realized that they would have little control over something that was so beyond their comprehension. With little control over it but with access to its beauty, they learned, perhaps, that such a wonder is not controlled but befriended. And when befriended, it yields its resources freely.

Like the Grand Canyon, the diversity of our society is a vast and complex wonder that cannot be ignored. Unlike this canyon which is fixed in place and quite distinctive, diversity is widespread and its distinctiveness is not always apparent. Diversity permeates the population to such an extent that those who are exposed to it soon realize how little they understand it. Indeed, many of the same ideas that emerge when one thinks about conquering a phenomenon as big as the Grand Canyon also surface when people are faced with the challenge of coming to grips with diversity. Perhaps it is best to realize that diversity may not be something with which we come to grips, except by standing in awe of its majesty while simultaneously working to befriend it. To befriend implies a belief that people of diverse cultures can connect in order to learn about and appreciate each other's personhood, artifacts, and ideas.

How Does One Build Connections?

I'd like to suggest that effective connections are built upon the humanity that we share. Effective connections grow through every encounter, one at a time, with each one building on the previous one to form a strong foundation of trust and respect. Such a foundation must carefully consider the entire context because each part of the base contributes to the quality of subsequent connections. The diverse facets of the context cohere as they contribute to the uniqueness of the foundation. Sometimes they connect comfortably, at other times the connection is awkward. Diverse facets dominate at times and recede at others. A spirit of reciprocity and trust emerges as connections are firmly established proving the adage that the whole is greater than the sum of all its parts.

An alternative image of building connections is frequently presented in the form of a bridge. A bridge essentially connects two or more points across a gap. By its nature, the bridge bypasses much of the abyss it spans. Also, it is selective. The points of contact and their close surroundings benefit from being within the pale, enjoying ease of access. Areas beyond these points receive less attention and fall into obscurity. As populations struggle for access to equitable goods and services, emotions run high when desires are not satisfied, and a sense of distrust spreads. Connections are difficult and rather tenuous if any are built at all.

Conversations about teaching and learning in culturally diverse schools and classrooms frequently refer to metaphors such as these. I am attracted more to the metaphor of building connections than to the idea of bridging a gap because the image conjured by the term *gap* conveys the sense of a deficit, an inadequacy, something that must be fixed or overcome. Indeed, student achievement levels do frequently reveal the gap that exists actual demonstration of skills and knowledge and local or national norms.

This gap is a reality. Acknowledging it, however, often leads to negative judgments about students and their backgrounds, traditions, and abilities. Judgments of this nature become liabilities, especially when those students whose test scores and classroom performance indicate deficient academic achievement are discussed as if they are personally deficient, or they are the problem itself. Such judgments also create the impression that these students are unable to help themselves, to participate in deciding solutions that would address their needs. Thus, solutions are sought in isolation and decided on by an exclusive group. Like the bridge that spans a gap, such solutions frequently bypass genuine needs in search of more secure footing. The students who have academic deficits are most likely caught somewhere along the periphery but may not be at the point of contact where the necessary intervention is applied. Or, the intervention just doesn't fit the real needs. The result is that the solutions, although well-intentioned, may render the students more disadvantaged and powerless than they were originally.

A word of caution is warranted here. It may appear that I am negating the value of the wisdom that has accumulated during years of effective educational endeavors in this society. I may even seem to imply that I favor a policy that would let students and families sink or swim. Both of these would misrepresent my ideas. Effective decisions that lead to change grow out of a process that is characterized by inclusion and the involvement of persons representing educational professionals and students' families and neighborhood folk. No one should be surprised that those affected by change ought to participate in creating it. Our democracy emerged as its earliest immigrants fought for independence from governments that tried to control them. Yet, these very people and their successors imposed restrictions on the indigenous natives that remain to this day in conflict with the notion of participation. A better approach to change must be found.

Acknowledging Our Shared Humanity

The idea of building connections, on the other hand, acknowledges the potential of people to participate in creating their world. It offers the possibility of something shared, even when differences in perspectives, attitudes, and practices are evident. An essential part of building connections is the recognition that we are engaged in the search for our truth and that each of us has a piece of the ultimate truth that unites us in spite of our differences. In this search for truth we uncover contradictions in our system of education and in our own lives as we raise questions about teachers and learners. How do they search for meaning in their lives? What is their sense of identity? How do they understand the unique and inherent values, beliefs, and traditions of cultures? How do they respond to cultural diversity?

Teachers want to connect with learners personally as well as academically. Effective teachers know intuitively that the choice is not one over the other, but "is dependent on a confluence of interpretations, ideology and practices" (Cochran-Smith, 1997, p. 30). It is through this combination that the desired outcome of high learning standards is communicated and maintained. Do teachers build connections or bridge a gap?

Coming To Awareness
In the process of connecting, multiple realities are encountered—one's own and that of others. Efforts to build connections lead to the unique construction of a redefined reality. This is not a simple idea to subscribe to, yet it is just what teachers who successfully encounter the complexities of a diverse society do each day. It is similar, I believe, to what Freire (1970) calls "conscientização ... the deepening of the attitude of awareness characteristic of all emergence" (p. 101). The way I interpret Freire's meaning is that the clarity of the vision we have of our students is in direct proportion to the depth of our awareness of their potential and of our limitations.

How do teachers achieve conscientização? They do so when they examine their personal beliefs and values and become awakened to ways that these have been shaped by their lifelong experiences with family, culture, and society. Having been awakened to these experiences, teachers must then examine their professional practices or educational contexts for evidence of unequal relationships, prejudicial attitudes, and behaviors that discriminate on the basis of any of the aspects of diversity that we have already identified. They also check for evidence of abusive use of power and control, and other forms of offensive behaviors and attitudes that demean others. If and when these practices are uncovered, teachers work to change or transform them into their more desirable counterparts.

Conscientização happens when teachers assess whether they consider cultures, races, or languages different from their own to be obstacles or enhancements to learning. How do teachers transform their negative attitudes into positive thoughts about treating all children in ways that will allow them to achieve their potential? Some teachers say they would treat all learners as they would their own children. Such a sentiment, while attractive, can also be patronizing and presumptuous. The reality is that human needs remain constant but how they are expressed and gratified does not necessarily transfer across cultures, traditions, and races. So, the best wisdom tells us to treat all learners according to what is best for them. Learning to do that presents a sufficient challenge. When teachers acknowledge that issues of power, violence, and alienation are having a critical effect on educational policies, practices, and institutions, they are demonstrating conscientização. Teachers can challenge existing conditions while being fully cognizant that institutional and societal change is the most difficult to achieve, but they are most effective when they challenge themselves toward greater awareness of these detrimental factors.

Listening
When teachers really listen to the voices of the learners they can create relevant discussions about the world of ideas and challenging lessons in which skills are mastered and values are clarified. To achieve that, two aspects of communication are essential. One is the language teachers use with students in conversation, for instruction or correction. Choice of language and tone of voice indicate how the speaker reverences the intelligence, integrity, and sociability of youngsters. The second aspect is how teachers listen to learners and encourage them to expand on their ideas or to project into their untested facets. Teachers who listen well speak less but more effectively. Having heard the extent of the knowledge possessed by learners, such teachers assume the role of guide in building connections, linking ideas, and challenging students to make better sense of their lives in this society. These teachers, who understand the essential nature of communication and who practice it, demonstrate a level of conscientização that is admirable.

Conscientização, then, is both the motivator for building connections and the product of building them. It is a quest that takes us through an examination—or analysis—of the contexts and situations of our lives with a critical third eye and a similarly critical third ear. This is a journey that results in enhanced insight into the people, events, and places of our lives and awareness of ourselves as connection-builders. While the journey is focused on people, attitudes, and behaviors, it is multifaceted, opening wide vistas for discovery. I discovered much about building connections during personal experiences with travel, teaching, and work in schools where the population was culturally and racially diverse.

Knowing How We Think
Building connections challenged me in many ways during a sabbatical several years ago when I traveled to Pakistan, India, and Japan, countries and cultures distantly removed from my own. After that experience I wrote,

> I have traveled alone to various destinations in the United States of America. I have also traveled alone to Peru, a more challenging yet reasonable venture. Circling the globe, however, staggers my imagination yet. Something is to be said about one's place in the family, the community, the ministry, where one is relatively autonomous yet known and valued. How the perspective changes during travel when the familiar supports are absent. (Cunningham, 1989)

Looking back at this reflection, I understand to a greater extent that it was not so much traveling alone that scared me. Rather, my discomfort was due to the fact that I was traveling alone through countries where languages and customs differed vastly from what I was accustomed to. My circle of support, my family, friends, and community were far away. Such experiences were unsettling but they did allow me to come to wonderfully useful understandings about myself, my ability to connect with people, and the difficulties I experienced in the process.

At times during my travels I was annoyed at being taken advantage of by taxi drivers who charged double the fare that showed on the meter. I was frustrated at my inability to read signs, to understand what people were telling me, to express an idea, to identify a destination, to share an observation. I was challenged to trust that strangers would direct me to the correct bus, let me know when I should get off, charge the appropriate fare (Cunningham, 1989). In spite of these realities, I had to create connections so that I might survive during travel. I recognize now that the connections were quite tenuous because I was in a survival mode. I felt strong urges to give in to fear and to retreat to more familiar ground. The irony was that nothing seemed familiar. I was stuck. A remark once made by a teacher about being comfortable among her own kind describes my feelings perfectly.

I could have been tempted to reproach the native people for their life style, which was so different from what I think of as normal. I might have deemed their ways to be stupid. I might just as readily have transferred the pejorative adjective from describing their ways to describing the people themselves. The path from thinking of people's ways as being stupid to thinking of people themselves as being inferior is a short one. Inferiority and invalidity become synonymous along this path.

Juxtaposition of ideas such as these occurs even before our consciousness catches up with how we hastily label situations and people. Consciousness of this sort never awakens in those who are absolutely convinced of the correctness of their ways. According to Wurzel (1988), such behavior is representative of ethnocentrism, "a world view which holds that one's group lies at the center of everything, and that all other groups are rated with reference to one's own" (p. 6). In this ethnocentric mode, we act out of the perspective that we know best, tending to believe that it is the best. Indeed, it might be the best for us. In some societies that are less diverse than that of the United States, ethnocentric behavior may not be so dangerous. But to impose on others what we consider to be our best way of doing and being is invasive. It does violence to identity and to spirit. It also denies a basic value of our democracy, namely, self-determination.

Ethnocentrism. Monocultural or ethnocentric thinking is an outgrowth of ignorance. Ignorance fuels fear, fear fosters isolation, isolation engenders division. The inherent danger in this thinking is the violent behavior it promotes. The current rash of hate crimes against persons because of their race, gender, religion, sexual orientation, or ethnicity should warn the society in general and teachers in particular of the need to challenge unexamined ethnocentric perspectives. Hatred fosters separation, alienation, violence, and, in some instances, elimination of those who represent difference. Only a personal transformation will move people out of such an ethnocentric cycle of violent hatred.

It is insufficient to simply state that ethnocentrism shatters connections and is thus an undesirable state of mind that should be avoided. The building of connections must be accomplished through a two-pronged approach that includes negating the undesirable while encouraging the desirable. I suggest that the desirable alternative to ethnocentrism is a multicultural perspective in which we seek self-knowledge while simultaneously attempting to learn about the reality of others (Wurzel, 1988). An interesting realization is that the greater the difference between these realities, the greater the ensuing conflict, and, hence, the greater impetus to navigate through this conflict with others who are experiencing the same phenomenon. Throughout this process we gain an appreciation of the dynamics of human nature.

Multiculturalism. Moving toward a multicultural perspective is essential for any progress in building connections. It requires us to appreciate and value the diversity of our society and to acknowledge the worth of human beings from all cultures, without placing value judgments on any (Greer, 1994). It requires us to acknowledge our needs and summon our strengths to engage in cross-cultural contact, including direct or indirect experiences with cultural groups that differ from our own. Cross-cultural contact—an essential component of progress toward a multicultural perspective—is marked by cultural conflict and disequilibrium as people consciously, cooperatively, and willingly agree to the process of connecting.

In retrospect, I know that I was experiencing disequilibrium regularly as I traveled. Although I did not know twelve years ago what I know now about the development of a multicultural perspective, I was aware of tremendous discomfort. I never thought of cross-cultural contact as an identifiable phase in the process of developing such a perspective. I wouldn't have used the term *cultural conflict* because I didn't know it existed. This doesn't mean I didn't experience it.

Is it important to be able to label these phases? I think it is. We need descriptive, judgment-neutral terms within a logical paradigm to talk about experiences. Otherwise, we might get trapped by the rhetoric of political correctness, using appropriate non-offensive vocabulary, verbiage so trite that it is rendered meaningless. Using politically correct terminology may be appropriate if some neophytes haven't yet learned appropriate ways to address or speak of others. It may help to eliminate disparaging comments, but those who use it should be aware that it expresses nothing pertinent about critically important topics. It definitely curtails the building of connections.

When I was faced with the cross-cultural contact I described earlier, I took what I thought was the easy way out. As it turned out, it was most effective. What I did was to step back and relax, and acknowledge that I had several supports in reserve. This very simple act helped, although it came to me serendipitously. I did not have a plan that said, "When scared, sit back and relax." But when I did take the time to look around, I noticed that many other people were traveling safely and conducting their business satisfactorily. Thus, I was able to allay my fears. I distinctly remember coordinating two contradictory ideas. One was that I had to survive. The other was that I would survive, but only with the help of these strangers.

Survive I did, but I doubt that I had built anything except very tenuous connections in this survival mode. Such a mode is characterized by being always on the alert and feeling extreme anxiety, by anticipating failure, by missing or misreading essential signs and becoming disoriented, by focusing attention too narrowly, and by being minimally prepared for the anticipated and unprepared for the unanticipated. Yet, this condition plays an important role in cross-cultural encounters. Behaviors such as these lead to some resolution of the cultural conflict in rare encounters, simply because the need for relief is so great. Sometimes they lead to correct choices. And sometimes they forge connections.

I realized that my experiences were similar to those of immigrants who must navigate the complexity of life in the United States. Thoughts about the immigrants came to me regularly as I tried to reach my destination. How grateful I would have been to find even one aspect of life that was similar to what I had left behind!

I also realized from these experiences the enormous task that teachers must undertake to orientate immigrant or non-English-speaking children who come into their already overcrowded classrooms. As I write this I am reminded of the extraordinary efforts made by a friend of mine who is a public school teacher in New York City. For several years she had in her class children from an Asian country and she took it upon herself to ease the transition not only for the children but also their families. She took them shopping, taught them how to use the subway and bus maps and routes, and even spent a night in the emergency room when they were involved in an accident. Very soon these people were sufficiently confident about navigating the paths of life in New York City and became independent. But my friend has very grateful Asian families and they remain in contact. Many are the untold tales of teachers whose respectful manner has eased children's transition into this society while simultaneously advancing their mastery of school-related subjects.

Teachers who may need help in developing similar attitudes and abilities would benefit from considering the following questions: How do they think of such children? Do they think of them as potential discipline and learning problems? Do they think of their inability to speak English as an obstacle to learning that cannot be overcome? Do teachers think about such children from an ethnocentric perspective that confuses different with wrong? Do teachers acknowledge that cultural conflict is an interpersonal affair? Do teachers feel threatened by the expectations placed on them to teach these children?

All teachers, regardless of how they think about these questions, need to take measures that will heighten their understanding of cultural diversity. Regardless of the contexts in which they find themselves, teachers benefit from an assessment of their progress toward developing a multicultural perspective by being alert to the inevitability of ethnocentric thoughts and attitudes and by confronting them honestly.

Transformation
Like many others, I don't consider myself to hold racist beliefs of my superiority over others. Nor do I think that I practice discriminatory behaviors because of prejudicial attitudes. Yet, when put to the test, I discovered the need for personal transformation. Maslow's hierarchy does not directly identify this need, but I believe it is a real need, implied in self-actualization. Its presence is revealed during reflection on personal encounters of an intercultural nature. It surfaces when people find themselves in the presence of foreign things, be they persons, language, or patterns of behavior, be they in or out of their native country.

When I reflect on building connections, I situate my thoughts in my personal background because that is the temple of my familiar. The consideration of familiarity is important because it is out of personal experience that we redefine capabilities and create adjusted realities. In the act of identifying relationships and becoming aware of the factors that impact on my life, I discover who I am, personally and interpersonally. I can clarify the values with which my life has been imbued since its earliest days. I can acknowledge that I am a cultural being who participates in family rituals and traditions. Outgrowths of such a reflective exercise include the salving of wounds, mending of rifts, and a sense of well-being that comes from knowing from whence I came and where I belong. Secure in the lens of my familiar, I can be present as others do the same.

Sharing With Teachers

Soon after this sabbatical, I designed a course for teachers that would address the influences that society and culture impose on learning. My encounters with diverse cultures prompted me to create an experience in which the affective domain would take precedence over the cognitive domain. I knew intuitively that research about groups of people, about ethnic studies, about life styles, about language, and other related topics would yield enlightening information. Trips to foreign countries and the experience of the culture in an authentic setting would also be beneficial. Indeed, such formats abound, but I was dreaming of something of a different nature.

I wanted teachers to have the opportunity to connect, to be touched, and to touch deeply their own yearnings for satisfactory relationships with others, most especially their students, parents, and colleagues. Martin Buber (1970) identified this yearning as the "I-thou" relationship, in which the formal "thou" frees us to acknowledge the respect that is due to persons based on their humanity. In some deep recess of our being we are lulled into the delusion that in previous times our society was more civilized, more respectful of its members. But then we remember discrimination, racism, and the various forms under which these were and continue to be practiced. We remember that some members of society were and still are considered to be less worthy than others. We remember that our civilized society did sanction disregard for the humanity of its members and continues to do so in subtle and not-so-subtle ways. Indeed the term *member* was reserved for only a segment of society. Connecting to some of these realities is cause for discomfort. We must place ourselves within the context of being a member or nonmember, participating in a discriminatory practice or being a victim of the same practice. There is no easy way out.

Searching to uncover the truth in our history and in current educational practices can be threatening. Arrogance, self-righteousness, self-pity, and overwhelming feelings of helplessness, and sometimes flight can ensue. However, if what emerges in this search for truth is examined within a spiritual perspective of personal mission and belief in human dignity, these negative reactions will not pose such a threat, and the potential for building connections will be enhanced. Essential to this process is the willingness of teachers to critically and sensitively encounter their reality as much as they can and to consider ways they might transform it (Freire, 1970). Teachers who do so in a reflective manner and place where their privacy is safeguarded find that their resolve to transform reality becomes strengthened.

Transforming the reality of education is a complex process that is undertaken by teachers and accomplished through their efforts to build connections with learners in spite of the significant differences in the realities of each group. Transformation might seem to be unattainable given such differences. Yet I have witnessed principals and teachers whose desire to connect goads them to do things that may not fit within the politically correct paradigm. These professionals bypass the "yours and mine" dichotomy and build an "ours." They build an inclusive community of learners, parents, and teachers who reach out and involve community resources in the education of children. They waste no energy blaming the learners for what is lacking but instead direct their energies toward building upon what the members bring to the learning community.

The stakes of education are high. Teachers are expected to produce successful students in spite of the realities of an increasing culturally and linguistically diverse population, changes in the nature of the family, and a quasi acknowledgment that the whole neighborhood must raise a child. Education bears the thumbprint of many individuals and groups, not all of whom are altruistically motivated. When teachers feel a sense of isolation, of failure, of frustration, of powerlessness, their potential to build connections fractures and their professional performance falters. Teachers who acknowledge the threat these factors pose to their sense of well-being and to the successful learning of students can become empowered by their efforts to build connections. They can override impediments to face the challenges that are before them. They can enhance their awareness of narrow thinking and challenge themselves to consider broader perspectives, as did one young teacher who told of an awareness she had had about the narrowness of her thinking. It seems that at one time she felt that she didn't need to learn about cultural diversity. Because all the children in her class were white, she didn't perceive any cultural diversity. After some reflection on the broader context of her school, she became aware of her misguided notion that if students look alike they must be alike. She began to articulate an attitude of respect for people of various cultures and a commitment to the challenge that living such an attitude requires. She began to build connections.

In this chapter I have set forth the idea of building connections between teachers and the increasingly culturally diverse population of learners who attend schools in the United States. The process emphasizes an attitude of reverence for the inherent dignity and potential of each person. It acknowledges that all persons share a common humanity that can be recognized through their basic needs and their inalienable rights. It places skillful and respectful communication at the core of connecting effectively with others.

Chapter Two
Spirituality

> In this chapter I explore the nature of a spirituality that can be lived by teachers. I believe that all persons have a spiritual nature, yet I know that adherence to a particular religion is not universally claimed. Spirituality is like an inner mirror, marked by wholeness and connection. It connects the whole person with the whole of creation. We encounter spirituality in its plural form through the depths and dimensions of mystery in our lives (Harris, 1988). Spirituality is a ubiquitous entity, linking the "rhythm of rising and falling civilizations with the progressive spiritual development of the human race" (Küng, 1996, p. 117).

In 1998 I spent several months of a sabbatical working with teachers in villages and cities in the Punjab region of Pakistan. During these months I was aware of a spiritual aliveness that was similar to what I had experienced during a visit to Peru several years before. Perhaps the newness of the surroundings prompted such feelings. Perhaps my long-term desire to do missionary work in a foreign country was finally quenched. Whatever the reason, I acknowledge that this brief opportunity was a gift, a time to dedicate to a pursuit that was of extreme importance to me. The spiritual benefits I derived from this experience and from my experiences in Peru far outweighed any efforts I had expended in either country.

Perhaps one of the most significant gifts I received was an understanding that the best missionary efforts undertaken with native peoples are done in response to their invitation and not our initiative. We in the West have answers to many questions. We have resources that can solve many problems. We can bestow upon developing nations a way of life that suits our best dreams for education, economy, efficiency, but not the people of those nations. We can do great things; the greatest of these would be to accompany and support people as they pursue their own destiny.

I believe that reverence for the traditions of a cultural group and respect for the ability of its members to determine their best goals underlie a spirituality that people who work with culturally diverse populations need. Another essential quality needed by these same people is humility. Humility has many shades of meaning. It is a virtue that is frequently mistaken to mean weakness or subservience, but its truest nature is quite the opposite. Humble people are freed from pride or arrogance. They have a wholesome sense of their ability that is coupled with a willingness to use that ability without fear of failure. True humility inspires people with a confidence that allows them to pursue difficult challenges. Humility is a spiritual quality. It may seem to be the antithesis of what is desirable in a competitive society, but this is not necessarily so. It is an essential quality for teachers in a culturally diverse society.

My Spiritual Journey

After leaving Pakistan I flew to India where I visited the Taj Mahal. This wonderful monument to the love shared by two people is awe inspiring. Its beauty is never fully captured on film. I then journeyed south toward Shantivanan Ashram. This trip took me from New Delhi to Mylepour, Madras, and Tiruchirippali. Finally, I arrived at Thanipalli on the river Cauvery, where the Ashram was located. Shantivanan was founded by Bede Griffiths, a Benedictine monk who had a vision of a Christian community integrated with Indian tradition in a place where people from various religious traditions could meet in an atmosphere of prayer and grow together in mutual understanding and truth (Mabry, 1995). Every aspect of the physical and spiritual atmosphere contributed to the achievement of this vision. Bede was in his mid-eighties when I met him. His step was sprightly and his eyes sparkled with remarkable clarity. Without a doubt, this was a holy man, a humble man who, having chosen to live poorly by first-world standards, was spiritually rich. Such a paradox!

One afternoon I saw an elderly man from the nearby village. He wore only a dhoti, a sarong-like cloth tied around his waist, and he carried a tin cup from which he drank water. Banana leaves served as a plate for his food. He napped on the bare earth under a shade tree after eating. At first glance, I thought this man was to be pitied. But as I watched him, fascinated by his apparent calm, I knew instinctively that such a reaction would violate his personhood. In the United States he would have been identified as a street person and probably moved to a shelter. Not so in this part of India, where most people live simply, even poorly by our standards. But their human dignity is not demeaned. They are connected to a community to which they contribute and from which their human needs are satisfied.

These two men radiated a spirit that seemed to be undaunted by worries about what they would wear or eat, or where they would sleep. Their eyes shone, giving glimpses of a spiritual wellspring that resided deep inside them. To meet one holy person is a blessing. Meeting two is to be twice blessed. I might even say that I was thrice blessed because I had an opportunity to share in their life and that of the Ashram for two weeks. The impact of this experience continues to renew me. The memory of these men remains with me as if I had met them only yesterday.

My life was completely immersed in the context of simplicity and the daily situations of the Ashram. Accommodations were austere. My room was small. A tiny, barred, rectangular cutout allowed a shaft of light to enter the darkness. Simple vegetarian meals were taken in common in an unfurnished hall. We used tin plates and had no utensils. (A spoon was available for the likes of me who ate messily without it.) We sat on the floor. Water for drinking and washing came from a tube well that tapped the cooler water from deep underground desert springs. Visitors who had not built up resistance drank the boiled water that stayed hot in the desert heat.

Faced with these barest of amenities, I learned just how much my worldview is tied to my culture, my family traditions, my community, and my profession. The metaphor of an onion peeled down to its core so that it is freed from its boundaries best describes the imagery of my memories of this time. When the extraneous layers are stripped away, changes in perspective allow us to see more clearly what is essential for life. These essentials look so different when seen in the simplicity of stark poverty rather than amid the complexities of our multifaceted society.

Prior to my sabbatical, I had spent about a month in Peru with my dearest friend Maureen. Maureen is a nurse who has worked for twenty years with the radically poor people who live in Pamplona Alta, on the fringes of Lima. This barrio is situated on the foothills of the Andes, as they rise from the sea-level land of Lima. Lima itself is a beautiful but crowded city. Well-developed neighborhoods house people of various socio-economic levels. They show evidence of an economic growth that belies the extreme poverty in the barrios that surround them.

It's been seventeen years since my first visit to this desert land. At that time many families lived on dirt floors in houses built of raffia. Water—when it was available—was delivered in trucks that once delivered gasoline. The water was stored in cement troughs outside of each house and served a variety of purposes, including drinking. Maureen could afford the fuel needed to boil it for twenty minutes before filtering it twice and then drinking it. The poverty of most of the native people precluded this option. A utility wire ran along the main road but electricity seldom passed through it. The road was no more than a beaten path through the sand. Jobs were scarce. Women were grateful to be hired as maids in the homes of wealthy families in Lima. Sanitation was nonexistent. Medical care was a forty-minute bus ride away on buses that ran quite irregularly. Even the bus fare imposed a financial burden on those who had little money for food.

The stark poverty that pervaded the lives of the poor in Peru differed radically from what I witnessed in India. However, the spiritual effects of my time there were similar. It was in these barrios that I encountered what I call the evil of poverty. The poverty of the Indian Ashram was an essential element of the simple life style that was chosen. This is not meant to imply that no radical poverty exists in India. It does, and it is well documented in other sources. However, as I did not experience it during my visit, I cannot comment on it. Simplicity of life style is different from poverty and can be enjoyed by people from all socioeconomic strata in any part of the world. It is a personal choice and presupposes that other options are available. To confuse simple life style with poverty is erroneous. There is no virtue in poverty that humiliates and demeans human dignity. There is no validity to the argument that some people are less worthy than others to have access to food, clothing, shelter, medical services, personal safety, respect, and reverence.

The poverty lived by the people in Peru was imposed. It was not a consequence of a decision to live simply. Essential human needs were denied. One half of all babies born of severely undernourished women died before their first birthdays. Of those who survived, only one quarter lived to the age of five. Children died of diseases that are routinely controlled through vaccination in the United States. Tuberculosis was endemic. Fires maimed and disfigured people of all ages. Terrorist groups impose an ugly violence to an already overburdened people.

In spite of such overwhelming conditions and situations, these people carried on their daily struggle to survive with a resignation that lacked despair. The resignation bespoke of a time out. Many of these people had left their home, villages, and communities in the mountains, where they did live a simple life style, marked by self-determination and self-sufficiency. They saw nothing desirable in their poverty. It was part of the price they were willing to pay in hopes of a better life for their children. Even knowing this, I was still truly amazed when, amid all their suffering, they would tell me about how good God was to them. I was astonished that they could look hopefully beyond such devastation to a better future.

In such a context, my apparent wealth seemed to be impoverished while their apparent poverty seemed to be enriched. Such conditions leave many people from the first world disoriented, with fractured language skills and recriminations against consumerism and capitalism. The term *culture shock* doesn't describe the sense of personal invasion I felt amid such poverty. Although Maureen had shared with me her experiences amid these conditions, I was not prepared for much of what I saw. The depth of the assault on human sensibility is beyond understanding. The complexity of the situations and the multitude of people that create such conditions defy simple explanation or, even, blame. But truly this is a victimized society.

I visited Pamplona two more times, most recently in December 1998. During these visits and between them I was conscious of a personal transformation that moved me beyond the perceptual horrors of the human condition stripped bare. Looking to the wholeness of these people, I saw through their fragile survival to their interdependence and their determination, qualities that carried them away from despair. It was in this context that I learned the meaning of connecting and understood the virtue of tenacious hope.

The virtue of hope is in jeopardy in the United States. I have read that people ended their lives rather than face financial ruin after the stock market crash of 1929. I knew a young boy who committed suicide after he broke up with his girlfriend, and had failed his driving test. I read about a youngster who killed two other youngsters in school before killing his mother so she wouldn't be devastated by his actions. How the burdens of one society differ from those of another! How differently people construct their understanding of what it means to build a better life! How do we learn to sustain hope?

Over the years I got to know a woman in Pamplona who bought bricks, one at a time, and piled them up outside her house until she had enough to build a wall. Eventually she accumulated enough bricks to build four walls. Over the more than seventeen years I have known her she built her house. Windows now contain glass and are covered with curtains. The inside walls are whitewashed, and doors separate one room from another. Last December she invited me into her home for a meal. I was honored. It was a privilege to acknowledge the pride she felt in her accomplishments. Her children, too, honor her as do her neighbors.

Gradually the lives of these people improve. Although they are still pawns in the political, social, and economic upheavals that regularly visit havoc on Peru, their indomitable spirit goads them into taking charge of their lives as much as they can. They say frequently that God is good and their faith sustains them. Stripped of any extraneous commodities, they know what their values and beliefs are. There is no ambiguity. They know that their strength and consolation come from close contact with the core of their being and by being in community with each other. They are spiritual people.

Spirituality

Spirituality refers to the way that people make sense of the dilemmas and practicalities of living. It reflects beliefs, attitudes, values, and practices of communities, Christian or otherwise, from which people acquire and develop their personal identity and individual spiritualities (Woods, 1998).

I agree with Woods and also with Robert Coles (1990), who acknowledged the presence of a type of spiritual prompting that is not necessarily associated with organized religion, or church participation, or some other similar experience but is situated within a person's relationship with God. Within this relationship the spiritual, physical, and emotional aspects of daily life are considered to be worthy of respectful attention. Realities that we might want to bypass or deny have value, not only in and of themselves, but also for the insights they reveal about ourselves and our past. They also give a hope in the future.

Religion is an external construct, an organized body of beliefs. However, religion and spirituality need not be dichotomized. Hans Küng (1996) infers a link between spirituality and religion when he says, "We need not so much a mirror, which reflects everything, as a magnifying glass, which can concentrate our gaze" (p. 130). In an ideal context, and by deliberate efforts, the spiritual and the religious can come together within a community and a profession. This should not be interpreted to mean that members of a profession should espouse the same values and beliefs. That is not necessary. What is necessary is that the members respect each other's values and beliefs and live peacefully with the diversity. Teachers who value their students can encourage each other toward faithful implementation of effective practices that reflect and respect these values. Valuing and encouraging are affective deeds of a spiritual nature. Maria Harris (1988), in speaking of the spirituality of teaching, calls teaching a religious act.

Spirituality and Teachers

Teachers who acknowledge the role that spirituality plays in guiding their lives may adhere to various religious beliefs. Indeed, this book reflects my spiritual perspective, which is grounded in my religious beliefs that have been nurtured by my heritage family, in the Dominican order, and the Judaeo-Christian tradition. Because religion is not something universally shared, to focus on it could foster exclusiveness rather than inclusiveness.

A spirituality that is marked by such an understanding is most essential in today's multifaceted educational milieu. This is a milieu that boasts of high standards and equal opportunity and access for all learners. Yet it tolerates neither criticism nor blame well and it projects blame and responsibility outward when weaknesses are uncovered. The result is inflated grades, social promotion, falsified reports, and overstated recommendations. In combination, these factors create a facade that hides many vacuums.

Teachers are the most visible representatives of our educational systems and thus are most likely to bear the burden of such situations. Is it any wonder that their self-esteem needs to be strong. Self-esteem grows out of an interior struggle with complexity, such as that found in education. It equips teachers with the ability to distinguish between their personal limitations and those of the institution, and it allows them to name the arenas in which they can most effectively initiate change.

Self-esteem is thus marked by heightened awareness that comes from reflecting on personal experiences. To strengthen it frequently requires the letting go of attitudes and behaviors that undermine it. This is done for the purpose of creating a new vision and setting directions to accomplish this mission. While some people might say we count our losses and move on, Harris (1988) speaks of mourning when she says "we name the pain, face it, surface it, and then grant it burial (p. 58-8)." Mourning is an essential element of spirituality. It ritualizes change and loss and makes us conscious that we have chosen to pursue our mission differently.

Encountering Your Spirituality
I invite you, teacher-readers, to accept my invitation to encounter your spiritual self and to cherish and nurture what you find. I invite you to tap into that quality of spirituality that renews the energy you expend in your mission of teaching.

This is important. We need to have renewed energies to continue the work we have chosen. The challenges and difficulties encountered regularly can drain us and leave us apathetic, in a state of lukewarm indifference that leads to burnout. The public nature of education leaves few choices to teachers. Even what we think we should have control over, namely, the choice of the pedagogy we employ, is frequently denied us by those who think they know more than those whose lives are dedicated to teaching. The choice we do have is whether or not we want to pursue knowledge into the spiritual dimensions of teaching. If yes, the question is how do we go about doing that.

The spiritual dimensions of teaching become clearer as teachers contemplate and reflect on their professional contexts and the situations that they encounter there. The International Declaration of Human Rights and the hierarchy of human needs as articulated by Maslow (1968) provide the perceptive lenses through which teachers can focus their reflections.

Reflection

Reflection is a uniquely human activity by which we focus on a specific context to various depths and for a variety of purposes. It leads those who practice it into deep understanding. It prepares teachers to make critical decisions and to set goals as they pursue their mission of teaching.

At an initial level reflections are primarily descriptive. Teachers reflecting at this level write narratives describing the events of teaching. Goals for professional behavior that are set at this level would be routine and probably related to some tradition or external authority. Novice teachers who have yet to find their voice and authority frequently start to engage the process of reflection at this level. It is an appropriate place to start because it establishes a habit of accountability and it demonstrates a positive attitude toward continued professional growth.

At a slightly deeper level we seek insight and awareness into our actions and beliefs. Teachers reflecting at this level might explain what they do by referring to the pedagogical principles that undergird their choices. Even novice teachers with limited experience but with a commitment to becoming reflective practitioners can move into this level without any conscious attempt to do so. That movement is an outgrowth of the awareness that emerges as a result of the process of reflection. Goals for professional development would be related to the awareness that surfaces at this level.

On a third level awareness of subjective beliefs about contexts, situations, and consequences is revealed. Teachers reflecting at this level might question how their beliefs came into being or what underlying assumptions motivate their actions. Questions that guide reflection include why teachers persist in some behaviors and who benefits from their behaviors. Reflecting on this level is indicative of sophistication and confidence. It marks a transition from an "I" to a "we," from an exclusive to an inclusive perspective. Goals for professional growth set at this level would be based on reflection and self-assessment in light of this we-centered, inclusive perspective.

At a still deeper level of reflection, more experienced teachers can examine their professional behaviors and interactions to determine how they might do things differently. Those teachers are able to do that because they have more fully developed understandings about the complexity of pedagogy and of the impact that politics, culture, and society have on education. As teachers gain in self-actualization, the goals they set come from deeply spiritual motivation and are informed by a broad perspective.

Contemplation

At each level of reflection, teachers and discover the spiritual dimensions of teaching because they are brought closer to the spirit within themselves. Reflection fosters contemplation, a presence of mind that enables teachers to act in accord with their values and beliefs. Contemplation is frequently misunderstood, thought to be done only by saints and focused only on their God. In fact, everyone can contemplate, and when contemplating on students and the interactions of teaching, teachers encounter their greater spiritual source.

My personal experience with contemplation is that my focus frequently shifts from one point to another. If my initial focus is on God, it often sheds light on my professional life. If, on the other hand, my initial focus is on my professional life, it reveals the God who is in people. Contemplation must start somewhere and must be focused on something. What will that place or thing be? I frequently focus on some situation that remains with me and that usually surfaces at day's end or during a long walk in nature. When I feel too tired to think and my mind is clearing, the remains of the day come to the fore. These may relate to some incident that was left in conflict. They may relate to some incident that brings joyful memories. One or the other is a good focus for contemplation.

Spiritual Dimensions of Teaching

The distance created by time lets me see the incident more clearly or lets me enjoy the joyful memory once again. Either of these is a fine ending to a long day. The spiritual dimensions of teaching emerge in the process and the motivation for teaching shifts from job to career to mission.

I believe that the mission of teachers is to touch the spirit of their students and their parents and to walk with them toward self-fulfillment. This mission is a human one that invites sharing at its deepest level, the level of the spirit. Mission is the outgrowth of a vision, either a personal one or one that is borrowed from another. It is a motivating force that stimulates deeds of varying significance and requires enormous energy, sometimes against great odds. The value of a mission is that it is pursued in the name of a higher power and/or is done for others. This pursuit is a lifelong interchange between one human being with another's life forces, which is done to effect change for some higher purpose.

The need for the vision and mission to be focused toward a noble purpose, one that is geared toward the common good, cannot be overemphasized. Many people who choose teaching as a profession are altruistically motivated. They choose teaching because they genuinely like youngsters and want to work with them, hopeful about their future. They reverence human dignity and work to develop equality in relationships. They promote the common good among students and with their colleagues, fostering mutual interdependence, balanced by common rights and responsibilities. They focus their efforts on advancing students' capacity to access higher education, knowing its importance for both personal and financial gains. Accordingly, they design learning activities that balance intellectual challenge with personal success.

These mission-guided teachers are frequently reflective practitioners. They are altruistic, not self-centered. As such, they redefine some of the popular ideas that elevate the ego above the common good. They also influence their students to develop a global worldview rather than a tunnel vision. Together these teachers and students participate in shaping the world order of the new millennium.

Teachers who investigate their spirituality uncover dimensions of teaching and follow a vision that guides their choices, their attitudes, and their pursuit of effective pedagogy. The vision is lived out through their mission. They consciously ponder their professional lives to make sense of them, to create change or impose order where it is needed. They do this humbly, from an authentic knowledge of their limits and potential. They do so from a sense of self-worth, of gentle confidence, and of a balanced perspective.

These teachers know that their greatest sphere of influence is within their own classroom and over their own performance. Yet, knowing that people working together will create desired change, they invite others to work with them toward their goal. They know how to take risks and are not fooled by the myth of perfection. Thus, they acknowledge their own human fragility but when it is appropriate to speak and act—even if their words and actions are contrary to the status quo—they do so with a purposeful but gentle manner.

They learn from past experiences. They keep their memory fresh through reflection and journaling. Yet they live in the here and now. They understand that the past is gone and is beyond change. The future is yet to be created from an understanding of the past. They hope in the future.

They believe in the potential of their students. Rather than bemoan what these students may lack, teachers start with the capacities that students bring to the learning situation and build on these.

They believe in their own worthiness to accept the call to teach. They have confidence in their potential to develop the requisite knowledge, skills, and attitudes. They have a desire to be true to their inner promptings but will not be naive in living out their mission.

Chapter Three
Personal Influences of a Spiritual Nature

> *Everyone experiences significant events that mark passages in their lives. Sometimes these events are personal or familial; sometimes they are societal. Regardless of their nature, they provide a reference point for focus and reflection on how we responded and how we have changed as a result. The experiences I examine represent a multifaceted composite of personal, interpersonal, and societal events. I identify them as spiritual because they represent conscious choices that I make to act to respond to them.*

The decade of the 1960s was replete with social upheaval. Riots, strikes, marches, and Woodstock seemed, in retrospect, to signal the extent to which the values and traditions held dear by our society for the preceding decades were being challenged. In the 1970s we were grappling with the aftermath of the Civil Rights movement, debating the morality of the war in Vietnam, and investigating the Watergate conspiracy. Unprecedented media coverage provided graphic displays of carnage and deceit on a daily basis.

During this time I realized the wisdom of my high school history teacher's prediction that our challenges would come from rifts within our society not from any external attack. She was so right. Except for the Revolutionary War, which gave us our independence, and the Civil War, which we fought against each other, we have been spared the massive destruction that war inflicts when people's lands become battlefields. But we have not been without internal conflict.

After any turbulence such as that experienced during the 1960s and the 1970s a society must recreate itself. It must weave its fabric anew, incorporating slowly and painfully new understandings that emerge from conflicts. In the process, dormant ideas and hidden realities are unearthed and bared. The consciousness of many segments of society awakens to the domination and exploitation that can no longer be contained under a veneer of civilized society. Once awakened, this consciousness takes on a life of its own. It prompts various groups to examine their experiences. I think of this time as an event in search of explanations that are beyond our ken but that become known through living our life (O'Shea, 1992).

Federal legislation provided one form of enticement to citizens' groups and political parties to rethink a society based on full equality under the law. It was under this umbrella that many of the social services proliferated, assisting agencies that provided education, housing, and medical treatment to people in need. Public services agencies were redefining themselves for the challenges of that time. The private and religious sectors joined the public agencies in scrutinizing their policies and practices. The Second Vatican Council charged Roman Catholic organizations to reenergize themselves in the spirit of their mission as it was interpreted through the signs of the time. This council also challenged religious communities to examine their roots and to live authentically in faithfulness to them. It was a much needed challenge.

My sense tells me that the collective consciousness of people of principle lay dormant as they struggled to survive the war years of the 40s and as they enjoyed the good life of the 1950s. However, the cataclysmic events of the 1960s and 1970s burst the bubble of euphoria and forced the emergence of a new social conscience.

Awakening

It was within this context that a series of significant events within my Dominican community influenced my perspectives on society, on race, and on culture. My community used the challenge of Vatican II to revisit our roots and rediscover the spirit of our foundress. During this examination of our mission, I encountered some harsh realities about the good feelings and lack of fear of others that I wrote about previously. We reviewed our century of existence to see what we had done and become through the last decades. In so doing we rediscovered some vital elements that had been laid aside and forgotten as we collectively responded to ongoing needs placed before us over the years. We asked many of the questions that any group needs to ask itself at critical times in its history in order to sustain and reinvigorate its mission. We approached this task in a spirit of prayerful reflection, silent meditation, respectful discussion, and consensus building. I am proud of the effort and the goal that emerged from the process. I am proud that we broadened our ministerial efforts beyond education and child care. And I am proud that this group of women shared its talents, energies, and resources with so many.

It was during this time that my awareness of the spiritual dimensions of life and mission began to expand. A spiritual director once suggested that I read the Scriptures as well as *The New York Times* and that I watch the evening news. This triangle of perspectives opened up to me an entirely new vision of life as it was lived in the 1970s, and is still lived by so many people. The Scriptures and the media became reflective lenses that shed light on each other. As I began to apply this type of spirituality to my ministry of teaching, I discovered many realities that I had never found there before. This was an awesome experience that created a significant change in how I taught and how I thought about learners and their families. The fact that my community was engaged in similar pursuits provided very necessary support and I participated eagerly and fully in the process. While this experience opened my eyes to many previously hidden aspects of life, one particular encounter taught me yet another lesson. Actually, it taught me two lessons. One was about techniques that are designed to involve people in transforming processes. The other lesson, a by-product of the process we used, was about fear and intimidation.

As is commonly done, we engaged the assistance of facilitators to guide us through our deliberations. They taught us how to process and prioritize multiple perspectives, to reach consensus, and, finally, to choose a course of action that would be accepted by the membership. This experience gave me much valuable insight into effective and respectful group processing techniques. It also awakened my consciousness to the meaning of silenced voices.

On the day the process started I was sitting in a circle with several other people, chatting pleasantly while waiting for directions as to the procedure we would follow. Before I knew it, the chatter stopped and we were sitting in stony silence. My memory paints a picture of one of the facilitators putting us through an interrogation of sorts about the meaning of the word justice. Although several ideas were suggested, none matched the desirable answer. In a not-so-gentle manner he asked why no one from this group of highly educated women, which included teachers, social workers, administrators, nurses, and child care providers, knew the correct answer. It turned out that the correct answer was equality of relationships. I wanted to tell him that the ideas suggested were valid even if not identical, but I was too intimidated to say anything. And the fear that permeated my spirit remains in my memories along with the meaning of the word.

I had a sense of being forced to say what I did not know while being prevented from saying what I did know. I felt vulnerable and overwhelmed. My voice was silenced. I wished I could have disappeared.

This experience caused me to look through a different type of lens at how I taught children. Reflecting on the teaching and learning that occurred in my own classroom and in school in light of this personal experience of intimidation opened yet another path of awareness. Shortly after this event I began to read books by Paolo Freire. His thesis made so much sense. It addressed the myriad effects stemming from a variety of social and educational conditions and practices that he proclaimed to be unjust.

I also started courses for my master's degree. I took an elective course in human relations which shed understanding on the experience described previously. Prior to the semester when I took this course the professor had followed a traditional teacher-centered, cognitive approach that incorporated lecture, research, readings, and some discussion. However, when I took the course, the professor experimented with a different format. He guided our study of the theoretical constructs through an interactive approach through which we experienced firsthand what we would have otherwise been told in the teacher-dominated lecture format. While this experiential approach is quite common in today's classrooms, it was most unique at the time. The professor was sensitive to the fact that fear surfaces during participation in novel formats and discussion. This is especially so when sensitive topics such as prejudice and discrimination are discussed. Thus he cushioned the activities appropriately to minimize fear and enhance confidence.

I credit my ability to respond well within this context to the professor's manner. It was gentle, inviting, probing, and accepting. He let the challenge come from our forays into the complexity of the issues. Our voices were never silenced through fear-inspiring tactics. Instead we used them to share ideas, clarify misconceptions, and seek answers. The astounding result of this format was the long-term impact that it continues to exert on me even after thirty years.

Reflecting on my experiences.
It is obvious that this second experience occurred in an atmosphere devoid of isolation, control, and fear. We were not victimized nor were we taught injustice through practices that perpetuate injustice. Reflecting on the differences between these two experiences, I discovered the destructive effects of unexamined practice and the constructive effects of attentive, thoughtful practice. I began to realize how important it is for teachers to examine their professional practices for undesirable messages they might project. Such unexamined practices perpetuate an unconscious curriculum. Unlike the hidden curriculum, which is acknowledged to be concealed within the content standards, the unconscious curriculum is less well known. It is buried within unexamined practice.

Unexamined practice can cause fear to pervade the environment. Fear blocks the cognitive processes of assimilation and accommodation, thereby impeding understanding and awareness, necessary preconditions of acceptance and respect. These dispositions are fundamental to building connections with others. In contexts where they are lacking, connections are disabled. This constitutes a form of abuse, by releasing negative energies that cloud the atmosphere and create diversions and divisions. It forces learners into compliance, a response that may satisfy the teacher but that inhibits enduring change or desirable behavior. Change that enhances behavior flows from a personal act of will.

Understanding this dynamic requires that knowledgeable distinctions be made between many of the current self-tendencies that have been blatantly celebrated–elevated even–to the level of virtue by the media and through personal choices. These tendencies can foster egotistical perspectives. Marked by efforts to serve self-interest or self-fulfillment, they are frequently carried out to the exclusion of others. The term *selfish* aptly describes people who embark on such a journey.

Alternatively, these tendencies can also foster traditional societal virtues that serve the common good. They nurture reverence for human dignity through efforts to collaborate, to show concern, and to work toward building a society that is responsive to the needs of its members. They flow, too, from efforts to connect with others in a holistic and inclusive manner. They are altruistic. Because all people, teachers, and students alike fall somewhere along the spectrum between egoism and altruism, an understanding of the distinction between these perspectives is a necessity for teachers.

I venture to say that when the search for self-awareness is balanced with the search to understand the common good, the potential to advocate for the human dignity of all persons is increased. The key lies in each person's motivation to enter into a process that leads to transformation. Although a few gifted people seem almost from birth to possess altruistic tendencies, most of us have to work our way out of self-absorption and into magnanimity. I firmly believe that people can be led to greater awareness of themselves and their interactions with others through experiences that touch them deeply and reverentially. These experiences should focus on the individual as a member of the larger society. They should foster qualities such as interdependence, accountability, and a sense of responsibility for the betterment of the human community.

Teachers who seize opportunities to understand themselves and the tendencies of their students, who strive to develop learning environments in which altruistic virtues are practiced, work toward the betterment of the human community because they feed the human spirit in each person.

Schools are fertile fields for the practice of these virtues, and teachers are privileged to be able to incorporate them into their practices. The examined practice, when nourished and nurtured through reflection that focuses on truly spiritual aspects of human interaction, will promote connections between teachers and learners. Given the challenge of this obviously complex task, we might want to rethink the meaning of the concept of learning community. It is both an act and an ideal context for the aims of education.

Redefining My Mission

Having evolved these ideas through my own experiences, I was challenged to share them with teachers. To do this, I relied on my experiences in foreign lands and at home. My intention was not to set forth a spirituality of teaching or to discuss its spiritual dimensions. However, I observed how readily conversations shifted into a spiritual realm as teachers focused on respectful relationships and intentionally practiced virtues of justice and equality. If given the opportunity to speak about students' education and welfare, teachers will do so in a reverential tone that is deeply spiritual. As they think about connecting to students and colleagues, teachers uncover the spiritual dimensions of teaching.

We are a society that bans religion or things spiritual from our public institutions. But no societal sanctions can squelch the power of the spirit. Indeed, teaching is such an intensely human and interactive task that it is impossible to eliminate its spiritual dimensions. Although they may be ignored, they await discovery. They aren't discovered directly, but are arrived at as teachers learn to listen to the interior voice that speaks eloquently, revealing the deepest longings of the heart.

I also observed that teachers appreciate an atmosphere wherein they can discuss sensitive issues in light of personal values and beliefs. Such a climate is inviting and nonthreatening; it does not tolerate negative judgments or biased presuppositions. It provides sufficient time to engage the processes that enable reflection on lived experiences and the discussions and decisions that ensue. In such an atmosphere teachers willingly speculate about new revelations and their potential benefit to their students.

The challenge to respond to the need for effective ways to connect with novice-teachers guided my considerations as to the format and content for achieving this. The most productive techniques focus the energies on writing and reflection within a framework that analyzes central questions related to teaching and learning (Giroux, 1994). Doing this fosters attitudes of honest inquiry into the present context of education. It also encourages favorable dispositions toward change. These attitudes are needed if systems and methodologies that undermine human dignity or the process of education for a democratic society are ever to be addressed.

I observed that the manner in which the teachers responded to this approach was admirable. They undertook the readings, reflections, writing, and interactions with great seriousness. Not that this was unexpected. When asked to do something that will enhance their professional life and that is worthy of their efforts, teachers always respond well.

Teaching Teachers to Reflect
Choosing the content that I would present to teachers to help them accomplish their goals flowed naturally from my own reflections. Yet, the choice was a conscious one. Many existing courses that focus on culturally diverse learners offer a knowledge base containing information about the history and culture of ethnic and racial groups. They also address learning styles preferred by specific cultures and races and instructional practices that match these. Participants in these courses frequently discuss the ideas and consider how to apply them in their classrooms. Such courses can be interesting and challenging and can yield a significant number of facts. While there is value to such an approach, I wanted teachers to focus on the people who are learners and parents and colleagues. I wanted teachers to ponder the implications associated with building connections between peoples, connections that are based on egalitarian virtues such as equality, humanity, dignity, justice, and empowerment.

Thus, I thought it best to unite the format and the content through reflection that starts with personal writing. I generally ask the teachers to think about a personal experience in which they have felt successful, affirmed, or discriminated against and to write about it. I ask them to recreate the context and dialogue as fully as possible; to describe how they felt during the experience; and to comment on how satisfied or dissatisfied they were at its close. As they begin to write, a deep silence pervades the room. After some time, a unique type of stirring signals that the writing is complete. I then ask them to evaluate critically the experience they have just described, using the following questions: Upon reflection, what do they perceive that they hadn't realized previously? What do they think prompted the behavior they witnessed or demonstrated? How satisfied were they with the resolution? What resolution would they have preferred? How might they respond differently in a similar situation?

This analysis is followed by more writing about the insights they developed throughout the process. Each penetration into experiences leads to greater insight about their nature, causes, and effects. These teachers realize the value of such insight as they apply their learning to situations both similar and different. Willingness to seek clarity about attitudes and behaviors that sustain or interfere with the building of connections indicates a disposition toward transformation.

This is a disciplined effort that is not without pain or frustration. Nor is it devoid of healing and satisfaction. Part of the cause for these diverse reactions might reside in the use of the term *critical* to describe the nature of the reflection and analysis in which teachers engage. While the reflective process yields understandings and prompts actions, attitudes, and dispositions that enhance the competence of teachers, the term critical elicits strong emotional responses. Distinguishing between the two is essential, not only for connecting effectively with others but also for preserving potential benefits of the type of analysis I want to encourage.

Critical evaluation or authentic assessment of one's work is too frequently expressed in terms that imply personal censure or disparagement. Undergraduate students who are prospective teachers clearly understand the distinction between critical evaluation and criticism. They are not naive to the negatively critical comments that squelch enthusiasm, motivation, and risk taking. They recognize that criticism easily twists from being constructive to being destructive. Criticism that disrespects people undercuts their spirit and impresses their memory negatively. On the other hand, constructive criticism strengthens self-esteem and enhances the ability of teachers and students to be more fully human. It can free the spirit from whatever binds it.

Penetrating the depths toward truth. Coles (1990), in speaking about ways that the spirit can guide the understanding of issues, contexts, and intentions uses the metaphor of novelists who spin stories aimed at the penetration of the many layers of truth. This is what reflection allows us to do. Penetrating the layers of experience leads us to the truth. Teachers whose reflections allow them to penetrate the layers of complexity in their classrooms and schools will find the truth of their lives and those of their students and the truth residing in their disciplines. It makes no difference how we name this truth. Rather, it is how we use it. The solutions to many of the challenges and problems that confront teachers and students in the educational setting and process are found in this truth. Küng (1996) encourages us to maximize our own humanity by creating effective dispositions toward a transformation that is necessary for today's global world.

Education must be about the process of change. The very meaning of the word implies that as a process it will lead us out of something, out of our self-interests and ignorance. Very often teachers think that such change will occur in students who will learn the facts and details of their civilization. They are correct. However, teachers must also be open to personal and systematic change so that they can guide it toward some desirable goal. Otherwise they might be swept toward undesirable paths.

We can direct change when we make sense of the context and situations of teaching, when we probe our own needs and capabilities and the relationships that exist among the people in our lives. When teachers are consciously aware of the environment, they can affirm their students for who they are and for what they can be. In other words, they can build effective connections by enhancing the spirituality of students as well as their own. Doing this is an authentic and valid spiritual endeavor.

Chapter Four
Cultural Autobiography

> *Writing a cultural autobiography is very much in keeping with discerning the spiritual dimensions of teaching. It pinpoints learning experiences along life's paths. It heightens self-awareness, illuminating who we are and who we are becoming, individually and in relationship to other members of the culturally diverse educational community. Once started, the autobiography is almost never complete because the insights that it reveals heighten our sense of the other, reducing fear and developing in us a multicultural perspective.*

In 1988 I spent four wonderful months in Pakistan and India. Those times continue to reveal themselves and, ultimately, myself, and I will be sharing glimpses throughout this cultural autobiography. In Shantivanan Ashram in India I met Bede Griffiths. He was 83 at the time. His alert aqua blue eyes danced in his head. His nimble feet seemed to skip over the ground as a stone skips over the surface of water. His autobiography, *The Golden String*, reveals his journey toward becoming the person he knew himself to be. Reflecting on his experiences of family and church and on various readings, he wrote with an intense awareness of how they had influenced the development of his attitudes and values. Reading his autobiography prompted me to undertake a similar task. I decided to list the titles of books I've read throughout my life, starting from my earliest recollections. This approach turned out to be very appropriate. It helped me to understand some observations made by my Dominican sisters in Peru and Pakistan.

I had visited these countries prior to my visit to India, and for some strange reason I was readily able to pronounce and remember the foreign names of places and artifacts. At first I attributed this facility to my good ear for sounds, which developed as a result of many musical and linguistic experiences. It certainly wasn't due to a great memory for names.

My Familiar

Growing up in an immigrant family I often heard references to home spoken in the various accents of the Irish brogue. I've long had a lively interest in twisting my tongue around sounds of the languages I've studied, and around some beautifully precise Yiddish and Italian words spoken by my neighbors in the Bronx, New York. I don't claim facility in any language other than English and French, but I have some minimal use of Spanish. I also studied German and Urdu but cannot remember more than a few words of each. These minimal linguistic forays provide some explanations for what seemed to be my ability for remembering terms spoken in foreign languages. My curiosity was aroused, but as I pursued answers I soon realized that the greatest influences came from my early reading experiences.

Born before television was considered a necessary addition to almost every room, my early experiences of leisure included conversations with family and neighbors, playing indoor and outdoor games, listening to stories and music on the radio, and reading. In my mind's eye I still see my collection of *Golden Books* and I can feel the pride I took in counting them and arranging them on the shelf. They were my treasures. As was common practice, I received books as gifts for birthdays and for Christmas. The public library provided additional selections from which to choose.

I read many novels, but the classics never interested me. Instead, I read stories about pioneers in the westward expansion of this land. I also read journals of adventurers who traveled to distant lands and of missionaries whose lives were spent in China, Russia, and India. These stories activated my imagination and my curiosity and probably fueled some of the romantic notions that awakened my interest in the strange, the foreign, and maybe even the exotic. So it seems that I was not encountering strange names for the first time but rather that I was returning to something familiar. Of course I felt comfortable. The familiar is inviting, a source of comfort; it is home, even when it harbors unpleasant memories. It shapes our perspectives and forms a framework through which we think about and respond to people and events.

Probing
Although I didn't realize it at that time, I had stumbled upon the key to how we perceive the world and the people we encounter. Now I realize how important it is to acknowledge our familiar. It is the space in which all our life's experiences reside. It is the source of our attitudes or habits of the mind which foster ethnocentric thinking and acting. It contains the basic fabric of our culture and our ethnicity. These are human constructs. They represent the way people come together in society. They incorporate past and present realities and struggles to identify a group–who they are, what they believe, how they perceive, how they judge, and how they act (Gollnick & Chinn, 1998).

Culture and ethnicity are powerful entities. Many cultural and ethnic groups coexist within a multilayered society such as that of the United States. Sometimes they coexist peacefully, sometimes they are in conflict with each other. To move between cultures requires a degree of competence and confidence. The difference between what we know from our culture and the reality we encounter outside of it greatly influences our ability to enter into another culture and coexist harmoniously.

Factors That Influence Intercultural Exploration
Human Needs. One way in which we can understand our ability to risk coexistence is through the framework of the basic, common needs that are shared by the entire humanity. We may mistakenly believe that the basic need for safety, food, clothing, shelter, and a place where we belong, is gratified once and for all during early childhood. This common misunderstanding can lead us to believe that we are ready to encounter every experience as fully actualized, confident, and magnanimous people. In fact, we are forever challenged by new situations, for each encounter is different. Basic needs that have been well satisfied add a balance to our way of being, acting, and relating. They enable us to be calm and to respond gracefully and graciously as we face unfamiliar contexts and situations that might otherwise threaten our sense of well-being. It is important to be aware that even when our basic needs have been well

satisfied, we still can experience a healthy amount of anxiety and frustration, but to a lesser degree.

Being locked into our own needs. An awareness of my ethnocentrism became very real to me when I stayed in villages where wooden carts pulled by camels, oxen, or mules transported people, produce, or sand—sometimes simultaneously. It was evident when I lived in houses that were constructed of adobe and covered with thatched roofs, and when I slept on charpoy. It was evident when I ate native food, sometimes not knowing what it was but only that it wasn't meat. It was evident when I wore native dress, including the shalwar kameez, the traditional tunic and loose trousers of the Punjab, and the debutta, the head covering worn by women in Islamic societies. It was evident when I traveled on trains and buses, asked directions, and made purchases.

On many occasions I asked myself if I was the soft American. I found sitting on the ground to be uncomfortable, and when I was alone I used whatever was available to enhance my comfort. However, in a group I sat as the native women did. No one had to tell me that I lacked the ability to sustain a position as gracefully and quietly as these women. We all knew it, but they were graciously accepting of my efforts.

I discovered that privacy and solitude are viewed differently in many societies, especially in those where houses are small, and heat and light are scarce. These physical aspects influence a major cultural tradition in which household items and space are shared. Family life in such a society is marked by interdependence and cooperation.

On some occasions I really felt that I didn't belong, but I had nowhere else to go. Under the circumstances, I was compelled to open myself to the warm humanity of these strangers who became instant neighbors. In their own ways and without a common language to share with me, they helped me allay the feelings of frustration and anxiety that intermingled with the sense of awe and delight I also experienced.

I encountered similar experiences in Peru, Korea, Japan, France, and during a summer when I taught in Puerto Rico. The life styles, customs, and languages of the people of these countries differed vastly from those in the United States, yet I was aware that many similarities also existed, and I relied on these similarities to ease my encounters with the differences. Even in Ireland where I feel so much at home amid family and friends, language and customs, the differences I encounter take me by surprise. I am usually caught unaware when this happens, but when I reflect on my surprise I am reminded that it is folly to take people and their customs for granted. If I remain open to what any context will reveal and if I temper my expectations, I can benefit enormously from visits to foreign lands.

Changing perspectives. The challenges I faced during my travels stemmed from the different approaches to life I witnessed. My comfort level was stretched to a degree it had never before experienced. This caused me to adjust my ethnocentric perspective and to acknowledge that these extreme variations represent alternate ways of living. These variations represent the unique response of indigenous peoples to their environment, ensure their survival, and serve the people whose culture encompasses them. They are contextually appropriate. And my life became easier as I learned to use them. They are not wrong, they are different. These understandings helped me remain calmly and enthusiastically receptive to the newness I encountered. They helped me quell my fears.

Cross-cultural Experiences. The transition from ethnocentrism to ethnorelativism occurs with Cross-cultural experiences. These will be more or less satisfactory according to how successfully the ethnocentric perspective is exchanged for an ethnorelative one that recognizes the authenticity of cultural groups other than my own. Such an exchange is absolutely necessary if any progress is to be made toward harmonious living in a society that is replete with cultural diversity. But it is not an easy exchange, the difficulty being equal to the extent of the differences encountered.

Cross-cultural experiences create conflict of intrapersonal and interpersonal nature. The interpersonal conflict assumes similar forms regardless of which culture we are in, although cultural variations do exist in the way this conflict is experienced. It is frequently experienced when a person or group exerts pressure over another with the expectation of winning, or being right. Some conflicts of this nature are quite obvious, while others are less so. The focus on the person, even within a business deal, is far more extensive in some cultures than in others. Because I am used to focusing on the business aspects of my task, I am taken by surprise when people of another culture seem to focus on personal matters. Yet, when I think about it, the business gets done. It is not wrong. It is just a different way of doing things.

Further reflections on this topic remind me of the most effective meetings I have with students whose academic performance is poor. In conversation I discover personal matters that are distracting their attention from their studies. Once these personal matters are attended to, the academic concerns are readily resolved.

Obvious forms of interpersonal conflict include being taken advantage of, or being the victim of violence or abusive language. These offenses render us vulnerable and we become more defensive in their wake.

Reflecting on my experiences helps me realize how much effort I had to expend to resolve my own intrapersonal conflict to avoid letting it escalate or influence how I responded interpersonally. I was probably able to do this because somehow I realized that I was not the only one experiencing this conflict. My gratitude for the example set by the native women who accommodated me so graciously grows each time I remember them. Being in touch with such awareness helps me remember to be gracious in similar situations so that these also become satisfactory and life-giving for others who also try to fit in.

Multiculturalism. A transformation occurs in personal dispositions, attitudes, and behaviors through the resolution of conflicts experienced in cross-cultural encounters. The validity of diverse cultures and languages is affirmed. The contributions of various immigrant groups to United States society is acknowledged. The interest in cultural practices extends beyond food and clothing to the meaning of the traditions that these represent. A willingness to risk asking for information from members of a group fosters personal encounters and a cultural sensitivity becomes apparent. Such sensitivity is gracious but not condescending; is accepting of others but not self-denying. It allows the values of all to coexist equally. Such is the multicultural perspective.

It might best be described as a pattern of equality of relationships among people of diverse cultures, languages, religions, genders, sexual orientations, handicapping conditions, and races. It is to be celebrated!

My Earliest Memories
The more deeply I enter into my past experiences, the more I realize just how far back my cultural awareness extends. As I continue to probe, I realize how much my perspective has changed. My earliest memory of cross-cultural and cross-racial interactions is of a school trip to Pelham Bay Park in the Bronx, when I was in the second grade. I still remember how beautifully the sun shone on that day and the fun we had playing with children from another local school who were also on a field trip. All of my classmates were white; all of the children from the other school were black. When I returned home that day, I remember telling my mother about these children and how well we played together.

Probing. What does this mean? I'm not sure of all of the implications but I do know that for some reason I was aware of racial differences. Perhaps I was surprised that the experience of playing with children of another race was so pleasant. Maybe something I had heard preconditioned me to believe that it would have been otherwise. In the end I just had a good time and I should be grateful to have had such an experience at that young age. Maybe my interest in diverse people stems from that pleasant experience.

The act of brainstorming potential explanations awakens me to the various ways a situation can be interpreted. The combination of several valid interpretations and the pleasant nature of the experience influenced me to indulge my tendencies to engage in cross-cultural interactions. Sometimes, the opposite is true. Unpleasant experiences coupled with narrow interpretations can inhibit the development of positive attitudes toward diversity and foster actions and thoughts that lead to discrimination and prejudicial attitudes, angry verbal exchanges, and violent behaviors.

My Familiar
When I was seven, my mother gave birth to her fourth child. It was July, school was not in session, and my father worked long days. My parents decided to hire a homemaker to care for us children during the day.

Mrs. Filton came on the day my sister was born. Every day until my mother returned from the hospital Mrs. Filton made the two-hour train ride from Far Rockaway, Queens to the Bronx. She came early and stayed late. Mrs. Filton was a black woman, one of the sweetest, gentlest women I have ever met. One evening, as she was leaving for home, I walked with her to the corner and kissed her. One of the neighbors made a comment. While I don't remember the comment, I do remember wondering if I had done something that was just not right. I also remember thinking that kissing was a very natural act, something our family did frequently.

Probing. My memories of this time in my life led me to believe that Mrs. Filton's presence was crucial for maintaining regularity in our life at a time when it could have turned chaotic. The reaction of my neighbor, however, could have caused me to think differently of Mrs. Filton. Yes, she was hired to do a job and she did it well. Should I have taken her for granted? Or should I have been grateful for her kindness? Past memories influence enduring attitudes, behaviors, and values, especially with regard to diversity. I create the future out of these.

My Familiar
One day members of my extended family were driving to visit my relatives who lived in the western Bronx. The route across the Bronx went through local streets and into neighborhoods where black and Puerto Rican people lived. We were waiting for the light to change at one intersection when a young black man crossed between the cars (a unique New York habit). He was whistling, and as we watched his progress through the traffic, my uncle said, "What a happy race!"

Probing. I'm certain that my uncle meant this comment to be a positive statement. He was a man who showed respect for all people and making a derogatory statement would have been out of character for him. So I feel confident when I say that hearing this comment at an impressionable age led me to think of black people as being happy people. But herein lies the dilemma. The comment might be considered to be a positive one but it also can be a negative stereotype.

This comment perplexed me in later years when I studied about slavery in high school and in college. The songs that were sung by the slaves as they toiled in the fields were mournful, not happy songs. Pain was written on the faces of the parents when their children were sold to work on other plantations, or when their spouse was sent away, or whipped, or hanged. No lighthearted whistling was heard at these times. I questioned whether "happy people" was an accurate descriptor as I began to realize that these human beings endured intensely inhuman treatment with eloquent dignity. What strength in the midst of suffering!

Do we really believe that there is no difference between suffering injustice and submitting to it? In today's world, do we really believe that parents who have lost sons and daughters to drugs, road rage, gang violence, or any other violations of the human spirit wanted to suffer such loss? Do we really believe that parents do not want their children to have enough food or decent housing or a fine education? The misfortunes of some people instill fear in other people. Fear keeps people from people. Fear immobilizes. Too often, unacknowledged fear becomes transformed into hatred and violence against those people or those conditions that we fear. To deny fear's power is to nurture it, whereas to confront it is to master it.

Perhaps the ultimate benefit of my uncle's comment is that a significant adult helped me to think positively about a group of people that is often feared and avoided. Perhaps an equally important advantage is that it prepared me to realize that a seemingly positive comment in one context can be derogatory in another one.

My Familiar
My first teaching assignment was in a parochial school in the South Bronx. Once attended by children of Irish immigrants, it was, in 1965, attended by Puerto Rican and black children. The neighborhood subsequently became known as the "Fort Apache" section of the Bronx after the movie of the same name was released. President Jimmy Carter visited this neighborhood as did other politicians. They promised assistance to rebuild the burned-out buildings that attracted drug dealers and to revitalize once-thriving businesses that would no longer serve the local people in the 1970s and thereafter. And I was unprepared to teach the children of this neighborhood. I was not afraid to live in the neighborhood and I held firmly to my notions of thinking well of others. Nevertheless, I was prepared only to repeat the same pattern of schooling that seemed to work for me and the children who grew up in the 1950s in my old neighborhood, which was only a few miles away. A few miles and many light years away, a place where the majority

of the children spoke English or learned it very quickly. Many of their parents were immigrants, as were the parents of the children in my new neighborhood. Many parents in my original neighborhood were readily assimilated into the job market and the larger American society. Jobs and assimilation did not happen for the parents of the children of my new neighborhood. Through time and experience, I have begun to realize that Lady Liberty's torch burns with different welcomes for different groups in different times.

The next year I was assigned to teach in a newly opened school seventy-five miles upstate. When people asked me about my transition from the Bronx to a small village in a farming region, I told them that I traded the bongo drums of the Bronx for the cattle crossings of the farmland. The transition was much more than an unpacking of my belongings, however. It was an unpacking of values and attitudes, professional knowledge, and practices. I was in culture shock. This new environment, so radically different from any previous experiences of living and teaching, caused me to engage in some serious reflection on life and schooling. I began to perceive with a new set of eyes the way language and community values, attitudes, and practices influence learning.

Probing. In some ways growing up in my Bronx neighborhood equipped me to interact in a culturally diverse world. In other ways it didn't. The five boroughs of New York City have always been populated by diverse people, but my ethnocentric lens led me to expect that people of different races and cultures would chose to live in different, well-kept neighborhoods. Accordingly, Italians clustered in one neighborhood just as Jewish people did in another one. The Irish clustered in what was called the South Bronx, a geographically correct phrase referring to the area south of 138th Street. Hispanics and black people clustered in Harlem, an area of Manhattan that spilled into the South Bronx as the population of these groups increased. People who traveled on the subways knew which neighborhood they were passing through by the people who entered and exited the cars. There were no malls in New York City during these years. People came together in the subways on their way to work.

As I look back and reflect on the racial and ethnic profile of these neighborhoods, I realize that they were segregated. Yet, during the 1950s this was how things were. The Bronx I returned to in 1965, when I began my teaching career, was very different from the Bronx I had grown up in, or so it seemed. Had neighborhoods and housing always been neglected? Had my childhood sheltered me from these realities? As an adult, a teacher, I could no longer afford the luxury of ignoring them. A white woman described her similar moment of truth as an awakening from a deep white sleep to the racism that had never existed within her focus, but that became her focus when she adopted an African American boy. "When children of color become your children, anonymous struggles become personal ones with names and faces that you know" (Wolfe, 1999).

Awareness. If only I possessed in 1965 the understandings I now have about diversity and the enhancement that comes from speaking a second language, I might have taken a different approach to teaching. If only landlords understood that all people were entitled to well-kept, safe housing, they might not have neglected and abandoned their buildings. If only city officials believed that the residents of all neighborhoods deserved services similar to those provided in midtown Manhattan, streets might have been regularly cleaned and repaired. If only all of these factors had converged constructively, the resulting synergy would have forced the society and its officials to provide what was needed by the inhabitants of my new neighborhood. The result of such a force could have been enjoyed by both long-term residents and recent immigrants, whose values and traditions opened yet another chapter in the history of cultural groups in New York City. Perhaps such synergy might have prevented the consequences felt by families as beautiful neighborhoods and their financial base collapsed.

People with options flee such conditions, those without options cannot. Instead, they must make sense of the complexity of such neighborhoods and learn to live within them. Most people do this quite satisfactorily. This is their home and they make the best of it.

Outsiders' perspectives frequently differ. They blur the distinction between the people who inhabit such neighborhoods and the decaying conditions they endure. Fear of the neighborhood conditions readily turns into fear of the people and leads to a sense of helplessness. Educators and other service providers attempt to surmount obstacles that seem to be overwhelming. Unable or unwilling to teach effectively in such an environment, teachers might readily blame the children and their parents for school failure and neglect to take responsibility for their own fears that lead to discriminatory and racist attitudes and practices.

This is a very strong statement and I don't want to give the impression that teachers alone are responsible for poor academic achievement. Academic achievement requires cooperation on the part of all the other partners in education. However, I believe that only when teachers get in touch with their underlying fears and attitudes will they be effective in building the connections needed to sustain their mission to teach.

Educational practices that are effective in middle or upper class communities, which are considered enriched, may not transfer well to lower class communities, which are considered deprived. Enriched environments include the presence of museums, concerts, and theaters. High academic achievement is expected of children who attend schools in such environments. Children who attend schools in deprived environments are not necessarily held to the same standards. Yet, all children learn to navigate the complexity of their environment from the moment of their birth. Complexity exists naturally within situations and contexts; it does not depend on socioeconomic factors. Teachers who shift the basis of their expectations away from enrichment and toward complexity, find substance in the belief that all children can learn. Unlike pedagogical practices, this belief does transfer well, especially when it is accompanied by a willingness to enter into the life of the learner and to disbelief the myth that only children from enriched environments can be successful learners.

Reflecting on positive and negative experiences through the process of writing a cultural autobiography allows people to take charge of fears. It helps them uncover negative attitudes that are fueled by fear of persons, of cultures, and of races different from their own. It also motivates them to move out into the culturally diverse world. Maybe they will seek friendships, or visit neighborhoods. Perhaps they will travel beyond the country's borders, but this is not necessary. They just need to tap into their inner resources for the courage needed to make their way in an environment whose complexity challenges them to think beyond what they know and are comfortable with.

A Teacher's Cultural Autobiography

I encourage teachers to reflect on their own cultural background and traditions in order to raise personal awareness of their own behaviors, values, and attitudes. Teachers who undertake this task embark on a journey of remembering family members, long-lost friends, celebrations and observances, family traditions and lore, and stories passed on from one generation to the next. They interview family and friends to seek answers to questions, such as when and why they came to this country, what languages they speak, what dreams did they have for those they love. Finally, teachers examine these influences to understand how they have been shaped by them.

In writing her cultural autobiography, Fernandez-Cabrera, a native of Puerto Rico, described her introduction to life on the mainland when her parents brought her to college in Massachusetts. Learning to speak English was of primary importance and occupied much of her efforts as she tried to use it in conversation. However, she soon began to notice how Hispanics on campus clustered in separate groups according to their socioeconomic status. She did not want to gather exclusively with Hispanics and soon began to feel disloyal for not wanting to speak Spanish and for wanting to associate with a broad group of students.

She never felt prejudice until after she graduated from college and moved to New York. It was in this culturally diverse city that she was questioned about her light skin color and her ability to speak proper Spanish and English. She was taken for a European rather than a Puerto Rican and discovered that she was treated better than her husband, whose skin is darker than hers. This amazed her. In her own words she explains, "Anyone who visits Puerto Rico is amazed at how different people look, depending on who their ancestors are. No matter what the color of our skin, all Puerto Ricans share a common culture" (Fernandez-Cabrera, 2000). She goes on to explain that all are united within the same traditions, language, beliefs, values, and history. This ethnocentric view convinced her that she came from the best people.

As various groups asserted their individuality, Fernandez-Cabrera felt herself being put into categories not of her choosing. She is no longer white but Hispanic; not American but Puerto Rican; not middle class but a minority. Her children are also Hispanic although they were born in New

York, as was their father. She contends that it took many years to accept these new categories, and she claims that she had to do a lot of reflection. Yet, she remains very proud of her heritage.

These experiences taught her many lessons about the unique contributions made to this society by various cultural groups and about the dominant cultural group that determines societal values and behavioral expectations. She knows from personal experience how it feels to be different. She uses these understandings to encourage her students to move beyond the hurts of discrimination and prejudice, telling them that getting a good job is difficult for Hispanics but not impossible. She encourages her students to pursue an education that will open doors of opportunity. She believes that teachers who believe they can make a difference do make a difference.

Fernandez-Cabrera has used the writing of her cultural autobiography not only for her own benefit, but also for the benefit of her students. Having encountered her own ethnocentrism she moved away from it to a state of intercultural sensitivity. She values the traditions and potential of her students and encourages them to understand the dynamics of living in a culturally diverse society. Such concern for the welfare of the next generation is an essential human desire that can be gratified through the self-awareness that emerges during the process of compiling a cultural autobiography.

Chapter Five
Stereotypes

In the next three chapters I describe different techniques that I have used very effectively with teachers. Each process is designed to delve into some personal experiences in order to learn from them. Each involves participants in the transforming experience of heightened awareness. Awareness is both a process and a product of the reflection that raises one's consciousness about factors that foster the building of connections. When teachers use these techniques to analyze interactions with culturally diverse populations they are better positioned to build connections.

The following exercise was described by Nelson (1993) as an example of how perceptions can be overgeneralized. A teacher asked her social studies class where Italians came from and one child responded "Italy." When she asked where Germans came from another child said "Germany." When she asked where African Americans came from, the room grew very quiet until one boy raised his hand and timidly said, "the projects."

How Humans Think

Humans, thinking people, are forever processing new information. We have been blessed with marvelous, intricately functioning cognitive systems that assimilate or accommodate ideas, observations, impressions, and experiences into chunks of information or skills. These are generally readily accessible for use or application in the contexts and situations of our lives. Many of these ideas and skills become learned so well that we need not think about them. We just automatically access them as needed. Walking, saying thank you, or holding doors are examples of some automatic behaviors with which we are all familiar and expect to happen. As a result of these expectations we can live better lives and focus our attention on aspects of life that require thoughtful interaction or the creation of a novel response to the vicissitudes of life.

Given this understanding, it is essential that we realize that the very basic function of cognition, which classifies our knowledge and skills, also prompts us to generalize about them. While it is very appropriate to acknowledge the benefits of this ability to generalize, it is equally appropriate to acknowledge that generalizations can be transformed into stereotypes that only serve to demean and harm, to undercut the individuality of members of a cultural group. In and of themselves, stereotypes, which are generalizations based on observable characteristics of a group of people, are not harmful. Nor are they demeaning, unless someone objects to being grouped with others who are perceived as sharing similar characteristics.

Stereotypes are paradoxical. Negative ones are both destructive and disrespectful. Unexamined or inaccurate representations of people and groups are damaging both to the one who owns them and to the group toward which they are directed. Because stereotypes can reinforce attitudes of prejudice and prompt behaviors that are discriminatory and biased, heightening one's personal awareness of them is a valid and necessary task.

A Stereotype-Awareness Task

The following exercise is designed to help teachers raise awareness of stereotypes. While working through the task, participants experience cognitive and emotional disequilibrium. They become uncomfortable and are compelled to push toward completion. But the completion of the exercise does not always resolve their discomfort. Rather, it frequently triggers an inner voice of heightened awareness, which surfaces at times when it is least expected.

The Process

I dictate each step of this exercise one at a time so that no one knows what will be asked next. The first step is easy and is undertaken with enthusiasm. I ask the teachers to generate a list of diverse groups of people. Once the list is compiled, I ask them to name three people whom they know, either personally or only by name. This step is begun individually and signs of physical unease soon begin to be apparent. Working alone and in silence, participants shift from one item to another; they look around and moan. When I suggest that they work with another person, they do so willingly. Laughter is heard as they compare notes and share information with each other and with the larger group. After the names are shared and the blank lines are filled in, a palpable sense of relief pervades the room.

In the next step I ask them to work independently once again and to identify stereotypes associated with each group. This step is generally met with astonished surprise, as is evident by comments such as: "You're not serious, are you?" "You want us to think about them, but not write them down?" "I don't think I can do this. This is very unusual." "Are you sure you want to get into this?" I tell them to do the best they can, that it will all work out in the end.

Reactions to this task show through physical signs of duress. These are not unlike bodily movements signaling that learners are reading from materials at their frustration level, or are responding to test questions for which they are not prepared. When I ask participants to share in the larger group, the spontaneity that characterized the previous sharing is noticeably lacking. Indeed, if anyone does share a response, no one adds it to their list.

The next step requires individuals to identify someone they know personally who exemplifies or confirms each stereotype they have listed. Although this requires individual responses, participants aren't told to work alone. When I ask if they were successful in naming a person for each stereotype, they report that they could apply names to very few or no stereotypes.

I finally tell these teachers to cross out any stereotype for which they could not identify a person. This final step of the formal activity is entered into with a great sigh of relief. However, unlike the relief that came at the second step, this time it is not accompanied by laughter. Instead, some serious processing and discussion follow.

Reactions to the Process
This task causes significant conflict, disequilibrium, and ambivalence for the majority of teachers who engage in it. Why? On a personal basis, it invades

their sense of propriety, or decency with regard to respectful and acceptable cultural behaviors. After all, stereotypes represent feelings and thoughts that should be avoided. Stereotypes may exist as thoughts, but they should never be voiced. Deeper probing moves the discussion and soon some of the devastating ramifications of stereotypes are surfaced. These include the inherent unfairness stereotypes engender, the loss of individuality they impose, the missed opportunities, and the lack of equity and access that result from stereotypical thinking and feeling. They are unjust and blatantly wrong.

Reflection. Reflective writing after the exercise and the ensuing discussion helps the teachers to organize their thoughts, to honestly assess their feelings, and, in some cases, to identify an action they will pursue in their classrooms. This step is extremely essential. It enables the participants to exit from the exercise and restore their sense of well-being. The intimate nature of journaling allows participants to claim what they own in private. They need not share it, although many voluntarily do so.

Decision. This is not a gentle exercise, but the awareness that it creates can open participants' minds to a reexamination of issues of prejudice, discrimination, bias, attitudes, beliefs, and values. The result is that new knowledge can be generated about each of these behaviors and attitudes, and perhaps cycles can be interrupted, and ethnocentric outlooks can be changed.

Multicultural perspectives can develop in response to experiences such as this one. The conflict inherent in it makes decision possible. It requires honest moral choice, choice about what is right or wrong. Such choice leads to change, and that is what teaching and learning are about. Change in teachers as well as in learners.

Moments of Truth

A curious event that speaks to the challenges of connecting what is being studied to the lived experiences of individual group members occurred during one enactment of this exercise. The group of teachers consisted of twenty-six white females and one black male. While the participants were working on the stereotype phase of the exercise the usual tension was present. As I was walking around the room a woman asked in a very quiet voice if the responses would be shared publicly. I reminded her that any public sharing is done at the discretion of the person who is sharing. So it was up to her.

However, my curiosity prompted me to say, "Why do you ask?" As she verbalized her concern that someone might be hurt, the participant's eyes repeatedly shifted toward the one black male. "He knows," I said. At this point she laughed and agreed that he probably did.

What becomes clear through this experience? Stereotypes affect our thought processes, even as they are simultaneously produced by these same processes. Characteristics such as skin color, which obviously distinguish between persons, alert us to the dangers of stereotypes. However, potential dangers can be missed in populations whose cultural or ethnic diversity is not so visibly apparent. I recall one teacher's statement about thinking that she had not had the opportunity to teach in a culturally diverse school, until she realized that although her students all looked alike, they did represent diverse backgrounds, heritage languages, and family traditions.

Learned people tell us that we must critically probe reality by analyzing our preconceived notions about people, cultures, races, religions, sexual orientation, and gender. Preconceived notions set us up to see only what we expect to see or hear only what we expect to hear. A very simple example of this occurs during the final moments of a sales transaction in a store. In the past, it was common for cashiers to thank the buyer and to wish that person a good day. Although such an ending to a transaction is rare today, I still expect to hear it. In fact, I hear myself automatically saying, "You are welcome." As a result, I am frequently told by the personnel that they didn't say thank you. This exchange is more humorous than it is serious or dangerous but it does serve as an example of the influence that a preconceived notion can have on our reality. Other examples of ways that expectations influence our interactions abound in the experience of each teacher and each reader.

My Familiar
Two little boys taught me a very important lesson several years ago. Eddie and Tim were in the same first grade class. Each day Eddie came to school wearing a pressed shirt and trousers. His hair was combed, his nails were

clean, and his shoes were shined. He always seemed to be listening quietly as I taught reading. Tim's clothes, on the other hand, were rumpled. His hair hung down over his eyes and his hands showed traces of having done farm chores before boarding the school bus. He frequently seemed distracted. Indeed, he often interrupted teaching times with seemingly irrelevant comments. Eddie's mother frequently volunteered in school but Tim's mother was unable to do the same because she was busy with the farm chores.

Looking only at the physical appearance of each boy, I was set up to believe that Eddie would read and Tim would not. However, just as soon as he unlocked the code to letter-sound associations, Tim read everything in sight. Eddie struggled with letters and numbers. He repeated first grade. Most likely, he would have benefited from being placed in a class for special learners, but no such class was available at that time. Special educational services as we know them today just didn't exist for children like Eddie in those years.

Probing. Suspicion that is based on race or physical appearance or sexual orientation is a prime example of the dangerous nature of preconceived expectations. If our thought patterns have been formulated in ways that instill fear of such persons, we are probably not even aware of the danger these thoughts pose to us and to the others. They frequently prompt action out of fear rather than out of valid knowledge about the people. Violence is a common result. Certainly, no connections are built. Such is the insidious nature of stereotypes.

Teachers who take the necessary steps to heighten their awareness of the way stereotypes influence thoughts and behaviors will be less inclined to engage in thoughtless reactions to people and situations. Rather, they will become more effective in the process of building connections based on the humanity of each student they encounter. These teachers will also notice an increase in the quality and effectiveness of students' learning as it becomes more tailored to real needs, rather than to preconceived needs. They will also become recognized by their peers for their contributions to the learning community that emerges throughout the school and extends into the neighborhood.

Chapter Six
Analyzing Assumptions

Past experiences have a significant effect on the way we approach the contexts and situations in our present lives. They have made us develop a set of expectations, and we naturally assume that these will be met. More often than not we are unaware of them, until we have an encounter that leaves us dissatisfied. When we probe these encounters we uncover our expectations and motivations. Analyzing assumptions is a process that guides our search. It helps us understand why some interactions were pleasant while others seemed rife with conflict; why some efforts worked smoothly while others did not. Chapter Six describes an exercise designed to facilitate that process.

Recently several faculty members were talking about cultural diversity on campus and in classrooms. We had just viewed a film of a simulated classroom in which a professor was leading a group of international and American students through a discussion. Actually, he was attempting to do so, but his own inability to acknowledge the multiple perspectives and to allow these to surface only added to the frustration and conflict that arose in the room.

Conflict In The Classroom

Toward the end of the video, as the camera showed the students' faces and registered their perplexity, frustration, boredom, smugness, and bewilderment, we heard the professor's voice speaking to the viewing audience. He explained that he teaches critical thinking and that student participation in the discussion is essential for their learning. He can't understand why the international students won't focus on the topic. After all, they came to this country to be educated. My colleagues began to talk about the professor's approach. Who among us hasn't had the experience of trying to add discussion to a class lecture, only to become frustrated by our inability to do so and to retreat to the lecture mode? So the professor had lots of sympathy from this group of observers.

Students' Expectations
As the camera focused on each of the students' faces their thoughts were also revealed to the viewers. The Japanese student was puzzled by the professor's request that she state her opinion. In her country, students listen to the professor and state their opinion only after much thought and when they have something of significance to say. The Chinese student was similarly puzzled and anxious because in his country students never interrupt a professor's lecture. He felt that he was expected to participate in class by speaking out and he just knew that he could never do this.

The student from Russia appeared smug as she acknowledged that the professor had no passion for the subject, and the students who did speak in class had no facts. The African student was bewildered by the professor's apparent disinterest in his tale of how outsiders disregarded the history and tradition of his people when they came to build a bridge in his village. The Peruvian student was upset that no one had time to listen to his concerns.

The North American students displayed boredom with the various responses and impatience with the international students' refusal to be like them. One North American student claimed she would like to be friends with some of the female students but didn't think they would want to befriend her.

Analysis
As I listened to the remarks made by my colleagues, I became aware that they soon shifted focus from the observable to what was beneath the surface, from the professor's plight to their own experiences. They began to wonder if the experiences of the international students in all classes mirrored those shown in the film. At first they wondered if the students' reactions were tied somewhat to the nature of the topic. Very soon, however, they began to reflect on the adjustment these international students had to make in order to be successful. Finally, this question was applied to similar students on campus who sat in their classes everyday.

At this time one of my colleagues recalled a Japanese student whose participation in class discussion matched that portrayed by the Japanese student of the film. He explained that he initially assumed that the reason for her lack of participation was indifference. Further reflection opened his mind to considerations of other possible factors that might be prompting her behavior. He decided not to pressure her at that time but rather to be alert for an opportunity when she could contribute in a way that did not violate her cultural traditions. He provided a perfect example of the process of analyzing assumptions.

In the United States, professors generally assume that the ability to question and discuss orally indicates the extent of a student's grasp of the concepts. Thus, they expect students to participate in class discussions. This assumption and the ensuing expectation it bolsters are reasonable and appropriate. However, international students bring different assumptions and expectations to the classroom experience, and from them we can learn just how unique this expectation is and how class participation can be thought of differently.

Before saying anything that might have proven detrimental to the Japanese student's success in the course, the professor watched for other indicators of participation and determined that what he discovered did, indeed, indicate participation of a different sort. Thus, he expanded his personal understanding of the various forms that class participation might take. In so doing, he assumed responsibility for the assumptions he brought to the experience and for adjusting them according to the context and situation. He dropped the judgmental stance that can disempower both students and professors. He humbly considered alternatives.

The Analysis Task

The process just described is an authentic prototype of the technique called analysis of assumptions. My colleague reflected on a situation. He identified the assumptions and the expectations he held and analyzed them. As a result of this process, he now has a broader perspective that helps him accommodate the diversity of cultural traditions that might otherwise remain hidden in a pluralistic society. He also has veered from interactions that might preclude effectively building connections with these students.

The analysis of assumptions is a process of critical reflection. It lets us sort out the implicit values and beliefs that guide our thoughts and our behaviors. Assumptions are expectations that we bring to situations and contexts. Everyone holds assumptions.

What Do We Expect?

When we bring our car to a mechanic for repair, we assume that the necessary work will be competently done and that we will be charged an honest fee. This is a reasonable assumption. It ought to be held by every person who seeks services from providers. If such assumptions are not satisfied, we have a right to expect that the mechanic will fix the incorrectly done repairs. We also have the option to choose a different mechanic for future repairs. Expectations are expressions of our desires, wants, and needs. They may be vocalized or silent. They may exist on different levels of awareness, frequently catching us by surprise when articulate them.

Young children have expectations. They assume that their parents or guardians will love them, feed them, comfort them, and keep them safe. Children assume that they will learn how to read and write when they attend school. They assume that they will have friends and enjoy school. They may not be able to articulate these reasonable assumptions, nor are they able to advocate for themselves. They must rely on others for this. However, they do have expectations.

Teachers also have expectations. Teachers have assumptions about their jobs, their interactions with administrators and peers, and with students and their parents. As is common, adults tend not to be conscious of these assumptions. Rather, we pursue our profession and encounter our experiences and do what we must to live decent lives. It is only when we encounter some significant event, be it pleasurable or not, that we ponder its depths. We do this so that we might be able to figure out what went wrong or what was good, what needs to be changed, or what should remain the same for us to experience the enjoyment repeatedly.

Probing our expectations. I suggest to people who want to engage in analysis of this nature that they start with some reflective writing. When I work through this process with teachers, I provide a contextual prompt and ask them to write a response. The following is an example of one such prompt that I designed to guide teachers as they start to write:

> Think of an experience wherein you felt oppressed (or affirmed) in your position (school, community, workplace) because of your gender (age, race, class, ethnicity, religion). Write about it. Describe in detail the setting and the context, the events and the outcomes. Try to recall and include specific details of the conversation.[1]

The writing usually takes about ten or fifteen minutes. Afterward I ask the teachers to think about the assumptions they brought to the incident they described. Following what my colleague did initially during his encounter with the Japanese student, these teachers frequently ascribe a motivation to the student or colleague they wrote about. In other words, they judge the other instead of claiming their own motivation. If the encounter was unpleasant, a negative judgment is usually passed on the other person. This is a common response and is done without malice. It just highlights the need for critical analysis of personally held assumptions.

Through continued probing and questioning, the teachers are soon able to identify their authentic assumptions. Usually, the simplicity of these assumptions is surprising because they are based on human needs, capacities, and motivations. For example, teachers assume that students would want to complete assigned readings or homework. They assume that parents and guardians would be desirous of hearing honest reports about the authentic learning of their children. They assume that administrators would approve reasonable requests for teaching materials or trips that would expand and enhance the learning environment. They assume that co-teachers would accept the responsibilities assigned to them. These assumptions are reasonable and well within the parameters of professional expectations.

Once the assumptions are identified, it becomes possible for the teachers to articulate their expectations. Identifying the expectations sets the stage for analyzing differences between them and the reality that the teachers described. For example, a non-tenured teacher initially judged his department chairperson to be lax because she would not help him accomplish

---

[1] All prompts used in this chapter were designed by the author.

something he believed would benefit his students. After completing the analysis, he realized that the basis of the conflict was a difference of opinion and that his judgment of her as being lax was unwarranted. He acknowledged that he expected the chairperson to agree with his idea. He realized that he should have asked about other available options that she might have been able to approve more readily.

Another example refers to a teacher who judged some parents to be uncaring and uninterested in their children's learning. After analyzing the experience, this teacher recognized that he judged the parents. He expected that all parents would be like his own and would take time off from work to come to school.

Action. When the thought processes are logical and clear, appropriate actions can be determined in order to reach a resolution. The resolution must be aligned with the context or situation. It must be mutually agreeable, that is, both parties should be able to own it and its consequences. In the examples described above, the teachers judged the motivation of others. In doing so they veered from the critical element of the conflict. For successful resolution of the conflict they must refocus their attention toward the outcome they originally intended. If they want to plan activities that will benefit the students or arrange meetings with parents, they need to work through the details of each goal with others whose involvement is essential for success. Teachers who do that will create a positive atmosphere that enhances their chances for successful efforts in a less conflicted atmosphere.

How Analyzing Assumptions Helps Teachers

Three teachers gleaned wonderfully helpful awareness when they refocused their attention on their original goal. One teacher wrote about learning how to work with parents based on what they believe to be best not what she would assume to be best for their child. She discovered that asking parents for help instead of blaming them when things go wrong was a great way to approach positive communication. It led to problem-solving, promoted change, and instilled a mutual respect she had not experienced with these parents before reaching out to them.

Another teacher shared that she always thought of parents as being helpful in aiding with their children's learning, but she had never tried using the parents as resources for exploring cultures, because she assumed that the teacher always has to have that knowledge. However, when she asked the mother of a Haitian child about her cultural traditions, she learned of their struggles and the conditions they have endured in their attempts to enjoy the democracy of the United States.

Finally, a third teacher explained that the day he started to become an effective teacher was when he stopped listening to the myths about inner city children. Every student in his class lived in poverty, some in single-parent families, others in foster homes. He acknowledged that the culture of poverty makes it more difficult to teach but it does not affect the way he teaches. He expects the children to participate in class, to do the work that is required, and to aim toward high expectations.

These descriptors demonstrate the effects that accrue from taking a definite step toward personal change. It is most appropriate for teachers to acknowledge and change personal habits and dispositions, but it is inappropriate to determine how others should change, even when we are sure that the change would be quite beneficial. The example we give when we change ourselves frequently encourages others to make changes. This reality was expressed by a teacher who became aware of the behavior of teachers, including her own behavior, in the staff room. She always had considered her school to be a great place to work. When she began to focus on her conversations with other teachers she realized that they were replete with complaints or disparaging remarks about others. Now she walks away from such conversations if she is unable to change the subject. She realized that she will never instill in her students the belief that all people should be treated with respect if she does not act accordingly.

Spiritual Dimensions
Perhaps the most reverential characteristic of the process of analyzing assumptions is the focus on establishing the right relationships with others. When we do this we unleash something of their spirit that might have been held bound by our expectations. In addition, we release ourselves from blinders that create false perceptions. We emerge with a renewed

understanding of humility. We can imagine anew how to encounter others with reverence for their human dignity while we maintain our own.

Analysis of assumptions broadens our perspective from one that is focused on legitimizing or validating personal choices to one that prepares us to acknowledge the validity of the perception of others. It awakens in us the ability to be surprised by the spirit, to be open to what each of us brings to contexts and situations. As we grow in these capabilities, we become more adept at building connections.

Journaling. This process requires teachers to think about their day, to review their actions, interactions, and reactions and to write about them. Some of the matter will surface because of an unresolved conclusion or because it pleases, or because it baffles. Journal writing is a free writing. Focus on what comes naturally. Return to the piece as more details are remembered or as understandings surface. Sometimes the writing itself is sufficient for an understanding or a resolution. At other times, guided analysis helps to clarify meaning. The following prompts provide ideas about topics or incidents that can be analyzed.

> Write about a personal experience. For example, think deeply about a time when you felt empowered, or prejudice, or discrimination and write as complete a description as possible.
>
> Think about a time when you were the best student you were capable of being. Write about this, describing how you felt and what you achieved. Include any information that you think might be relevant to your feelings.
>
> Select one or more journal entries describing encounters with students, their parents, or colleagues that you want to examine more closely. Or choose entries that relate to concepts you want to explore further. Describe them as completely as possible. Fully develop the context with observable facts (not judgments) about what led up to the incident, what happened during it, and what followed it.

The responses to each of these prompts can be analyzed through a similar pattern of processing. This includes: identify the outcomes you expected to occur (these are your assumptions) and explain them. Compare the outcomes with what actually occurred. How different were the outcomes? How satisfied were you? How satisfied were the other participants? How might you approach a similar experience in the future?

The various types of analyses suggested throughout this chapter require a significant amount of critical thinking. Accomplishing the task is surprisingly difficult. Perhaps this is a commentary on a society that is generally not inclined to probe and assign motivations to another's behaviors or words. In one sense the avoidance of probing, and possibly presuming to assign motivation is a positive indicator of a non-judgmental stance. However, probing meaning for the purpose of understanding interactions and thus avoiding future conflict is a desirable type of critical analysis. Teachers need to hone the skill of critical analysis for it is this ability that helps us to engage more deeply in life. To avoid the practice of this skill is to lose it. To lose the skill is to deprive future generations of access to it. Very few aspects of life have simple meanings or explanations. They must be probed for the wonders they can reveal.

Chapter Seven
Social Analysis

In this chapter I model a limited form of social analysis using the Hansel and Gretel story. Social analysis is a process of deep probing into contexts in order to create and study factors that can negatively affect learners and schools. Through the process participants identify sources of conflict on various societal levels. Communication, cooperation, and inclusiveness are essential for effective analysis. People who are affected by the situation or the conflict should participate in seeking to resolve it.

Hansel and Gretel are two children who capture the hearts of every person who hears their story. They live with their father and stepmother in a cottage in a clearing in the woods. Times are rough and there's little in the line of food or resources to sustain the family of four. According to the legend, the stepmother decides that she and the children's father can survive only if the children are sent away. So she devises a plan to abandon them in the deep woods. The father, whose loyalties are torn between his spouse and his children, becomes an accomplice in the plan. Hansel overhears the adults' conversation and tells Gretel. He consoles her with his promise to take care of the two of them. Indeed, he shows himself to be quite resourceful when he gathers pebbles that shine in the moonlight and uses them to mark the path the parents lead them along toward their fate. His plan works well, and soon after being abandoned in the woods the children surprise their parents by returning home.

For some time they seem to be able to survive together; yet when times get bad once again, the children face the same fate of abandonment. They are not as lucky during their second trip into the deep woods. While

Hansel's resourcefulness served them well when they were first abandoned, his choice of using crumbs from the meager slice of bread meant to sustain the two children place them in double harm. The trail he creates with bread crumbs is eaten by the animals; the food they needed for strength is denied to them. Thus, they wander aimlessly through the woods until they come to the extraordinary cottage of the witch. Enticed by food, they quickly fall prey to the snares of this character and for a brief time they hover precariously between life and death until Gretel uses her own resources. In a sudden turn of events, this timid child pushes the witch into the hot oven intended for Hansel. Free at last, they discover a wealth undreamed of and certainly unknown to them before, as the house is filled with precious gems and coins. They manage to find their way through the woods and are reunited with their father, whose wife had died. They live happily ever after.

The Social Analysis Process
The Problem
The first step in social analysis is to name the problem and to describe it in detail. After reading Hansel and Gretel to establish a common knowledge of the story, I ask for brief descriptions of the principal players, because the problem exists around their lives. Who are they? What are they like? What do they do? How do they live? The answers to these questions establish a general understanding of each character. Usually the father is described as being loving toward his children but unable to contradict his wife. He is considered morally weak. The stepmother is described as being overbearing, greedy, and selfish. Hansel is considered to be resourceful and protective, while Gretel is thought of as being timid and fearful but capable of rising to the occasion. The immediate problem is seen as the impending abandonment of the children.

Probing the relationships among the players. Once these descriptors are identified, the relationships between the characters are analyzed. Discussions that focus on the nature of the interactions between the spouses, between the children, and between children and parents surface ideas that make the characters seem more closely aligned with people we all know.

The relationship between the children is marked by protection and caring. They know that they have to rely on each other for their safety and consolation, and they must use all of their resources to survive. Both must assume responsibility for each other's care in ways that their resources and experiences have not prepared them to do. The relationship between the spouses is full of conflict and marked by domination. Not only are they unable to provide for each other and the children, they also do not agree on the solution. Indeed, the father acquiesces to his spouse's wishes. The relationship between the children and their parents is similarly conflicted. The children can't trust that the adults who should provide for and protect them will do so. This destitute family must be self-sufficient as no societal structures exist to provide public assistance.

The witch is an interesting character to analyze. What does the witch represent? There is general consensus that this character is a metaphor for evil, and more specifically for the evil that pervades conditions of such extreme poverty as are portrayed through this story. Once identified, the reality of poverty in the lives of the characters is examined to discover its effects. Why is this family so poor? What effect does poverty have on family life? How does it impact the relationship between parents? What unrealistic demands does it make on children? How does it influence the relationship between children and their parents?

The relevance of timeless stories. The next step of the social analysis process involves a discussion about why this problem is being studied. For most teachers, the reasons are quite clear. Teachers who work with poor, abandoned, or homeless children recognize the reality base of this story. So do teachers who work with children from unstable families who must assume adult responsibility for themselves and their siblings long before they ought to. Although few teachers have participated in such critical analysis of the tale, they have no difficulty seeing it anew through the lives of their students. The universal themes and timelessness of folktales readily reflect the current reality that too many teachers encounter in classrooms and schools.

The value of learning social analysis through such stories lies in the understandings that evolve because of their freedom from conventional frameworks. The long ago and far away setting frees the mind from painful details and factors that frequently hinder probing. These stories foster thoughts and discussions without reference to politically correct, thought-stopping epithets. To enable teachers to probe reality, descriptions of the variables under discussion must be elaborated so that their contradictions can be uncovered. This develops confidence and skill in forming critical judgments—an essential component of connecting to the culturally diverse population of the schools.

Finding solutions to the problem. The remaining steps in the process include brainstorming about the causes of and solutions to the problem, examining the consequences of each, and identifying conditions that might interfere with or enhance change. Finally, the solutions are implemented and tested for effectiveness. If I were guiding a group of teachers through the process of analyzing a current problem, I would follow the steps as they have been outlined. However, because I am modeling the analysis of the story, I will devote extended discussion to the interfering conditions.

Application Through Reflection
Because it is essential that the understandings gleaned through critical analysis be applied to the reality of the classroom, teachers would benefit from considering the following exercise.

> Imagine being the teacher in whose class sit Hansel and Gretel. How would you respond? What background would they bring to the classroom environment? How might they relate to you and to other learners? How might you involve their parents in their education? How would you label them? What academic goals would you set for them? To what standards would you hold them? Would they have any special learning needs? What programs or instructional paradigms might they need in order to be successful learners? What would you do to ensure their academic success? How might they define successful learning?[1]

Beyond the classroom. Thinking beyond the actual classroom or school applications to the broader society, I share some extended thoughts. Reading a newspaper, observing motorists on roads or in parking lots, hearing people talk to each other in anger and haste, experiencing

---

[1] This writing exercise was designed by the author.

inadequate service by providers, and watching public officials engage in election campaigns can readily convey the feeling that something is seriously awry in our society. Hans Küng calls it a moral crisis, a vacuum of meaning that is distinguished by a lack of goals and of a sense of values upon which to base decisions. It comes about through the destruction and loss of traditions, of a broad perspective on life, and of ethical criteria (1996). Küng is a person whose background is steeped in traditions, both sacred and secular, and who was taught in his youth to maintain a balance between the common good and his personal needs. He believes that ethical principles can guide society and that society can expect its members to abide by acceptable standards of right or wrong, good or bad. Many of these standards emanate from the religious traditions adhered to by the people. When the standards, traditions, and ethics of a society diminish radically and hope becomes lost, children are the most vulnerable because they are the most bereft. What moral or ethical legacy does society offer that will ground them as the innocence of their youth gives way to the skepticism of adulthood?

A metaphor. These ideas remind me of nesting dolls, those marvelous creations of Russian artisans. They delight both the young and old, who eagerly open each doll to be surprised by yet another one within. The old laugh because their expectations are confirmed. The young laugh because they are surprised. The legacy of their experiences teaches them what to expect in subsequent encounters with these dolls. The larger dolls surround and protect the smallest one which is the only whole figure. It cannot be divided further without incurring severe and irreparable damage.

If the set of dolls was considered to be a metaphor for our current society, what would the larger dolls represent? Would they represent traditions, ethical criteria, standards of right or wrong that Küng believes are so valuable in guiding the young members of a society? What are these traditions, criteria, standards, and who passes them on to the young? Or, would the dolls represent the layers of society that surround the young, starting with the family and moving outward to the school, the neighborhood, the city, the state, the nation? How would these units of society protect its smallest, most vulnerable members? Hilary Rodham Clinton (1996) has proclaimed that it takes a village to raise a child.

Extending this metaphor, I suggest that it takes a neighborhood to educate a child.

By investigating the metaphor we discover how the structural level of society should assist families in the task of raising children by providing necessary services. Included among these services are education, housing, medical facilities, churches, and community services provided to fight fires, maintain a safe and clean environment, provide public transportation, and supply food, clothing, and shelter as needed

If you think back to your childhood and recreate your neighborhood, do you discover the village that raised you? Do you remember the neighborhood that educated you? Are your memories fragmented? I've already mentioned that although freedom and equality were cherished ideals of this democratic society, they were not universally available to all citizens and aliens. It is appropriate to acknowledge that the lives of all children have not been idyllic and that many children carry too many adult responsibilities before they have been properly nurtured to do so. The Hansel and Gretel story lives on. It is told today through the stories of all children–be they poor or rich.

Our children. The plight of poor children is visible. That of middle and upper class children is less transparent, concealed by the trappings of material goods. The plight of all children rests on the good fortune or misfortune of their families. It also rests on the access to services, public or private, that assist families in living a life that is worthy of all humanity.

Common assumptions about poor children abound, forming a collection of myth and reality. Some of these assumptions are that these children are abandoned and abused, that they are underfed, underclothed, underhoused, and underloved; that they are unmotivated, understimulated, and underprepared to achieve in school and graduate; that consequently they probably will not get a job and thus be unable to contribute to society's betterment; that they are also underdirected, undisciplined, and are destined to become criminals and spend their life in jail; that they are underdeveloped emotionally for the responsibilities they must assume and give birth to children irresponsibly; and that without the intervention of some significant external factors (a fairy godmother, a charming prince, winning the lottery, coming to the attention of Annie's Daddy Warbucks) their destiny is to remain in the cycle of poverty. It is important to remember that frequently assumed generalizations are just as frequently inaccurate.

Common assumptions about the children of the middle and upper class also abound, forming a similar collection of myth and reality. People assume that these children are ignored and left too much to their own devices; that they run away from home in search of something they can neither name nor explain; that they are pampered; that at an early age they have their own television, their own sound systems, their own computer hookups to the Internet, their own telephones in their own private room; that except for eating and going to school, they can probably exist in their own rooms, isolated from other members of their families who are similarly entertaining themselves; that they are overstimulated in an enriched environment but they do not understand its complexities; that they are not prepared to make the personal choices available to them; that they are overprogrammed in competitive activities and take lessons of many sorts from a variety of experts; that they learn that they are to be served and serviced; that they attend excellent schools and earn good grades even though they may be underdeveloped academically; that they are goaded toward self-sufficiency, that nebulous entity that is considered the backbone of the American spirit. These generalizations are as inaccurate as are those associated with poor children.

Providing essential services. It is appropriate to acknowledge that significant differences and similarities between children of poverty and children of apparent wealth do exist. One essential difference is in the accessibility of essential goods and services. Another is in the perception of themselves as being worthy of getting access to the best of these goods and services. Children who are repeatedly denied access or serviced poorly may eventually believe that they are not worthy. An essential similarity is in their ability or their desire to acknowledge that they are interdependent and not as isolated as their differences would indicate. All share a common humanity and none are perfect.

It is also important to focus attention on the many institutions that are authorized to provide services that protect the human rights and needs of children and that have yet to satisfy their mission, which is the reason for their existence and funding. Hospitals are places where people go in the hope of being cured of their illnesses. In fact, people do not necessarily recover their good health in hospitals. Courts of law are places where people go in the hope of receiving justice. In fact, people do not necessarily receive just treatments or pronouncements in courts of law. Schools are places where people go in the hope of attaining an education. In fact, people do not necessarily become effectively educated in schools. These statements should not be dismissed as overgeneralizations. Acknowledging such realities can strengthen the potential for improved services. It can motivate responsible agencies to take the necessary steps to remedy deficiencies and equalize the way all children are serviced.

We live in an imperfect society that has not learned to match its actions with its ideals. Conflicting agendas divert institutions and services from their mission of service to others. I want to suggest that institutions authorized to provide services that protect human rights and needs have floundered in their mission to provide services and enhance reverence and dignity. What does it mean to enhance the dignity of others? There is a story told of an ancient Indian teacher who greeted his students with a deep bow. This was how he reverenced them. Once we bow to others out of our willingness to serve them, other ways of reverencing become evident.

Several years ago newspapers and newscasters reported that the New York City school system was lagging behind in complying with the federally mandated removal of asbestos. Indeed, after a summer of inactivity, the opening day of school was approaching, and the job had not been completed. This is not reverence for the students and the teachers. Kozol's (1991) writings have detailed other lurid scenarios related to emergency rooms and hospital clinics as well as housing conditions that exist in the neighborhoods of the poor.

A true reverencing of others will come through transformed attitudes and dispositions and through visions of services that are responsive to people's needs. A true reverencing of others will become evident when equitable funding is allocated to support agencies that service people, and when people of integrity work together to create the best possible response to the needs of society. Such persons leave a legacy of reverence for the next generation to follow.

Spiritual Dimensions and Building Connections

What has all of this to do with spirituality, with creating and building connections between teachers, students, and their families? Quite a bit. The very act of probing to such depths and as broadly as is described in this chapter can be very upsetting. It can cause teachers to despair that education might achieve the intended effect. It can cause teachers to feel overwhelmed and powerless. It can cause them to give up. It can leave them spiritually bankrupt, demoralized, and depressed.

On the other hand, pursuing the analysis can open their eyes and minds to alternative solutions to problems they encounter. This is an antidote to demoralization and depression. The cooperation and communication required throughout the process can restore personal connections that might become severed during conflict. Engaging in such an in-depth process with colleagues and neighbors can create a common spiritual bond that emerges when people work hard together to achieve some worthwhile goal. Spirituality is both the process and product of making sense of a context, probing it for meaning and creating meaning where none is to be found.

Chapter Eight
Culturally Responsive Pedagogy

> *This chapter expands the rationale for building connections with students through a spirituality that fosters the development of a multicultural perspective. If a spiritually based multicultural perspective guides teachers to incorporate students' cultural traditions in learning experiences, the learning environment becomes charged with reverence for human potential, dignity, and enthusiasm for learning. The search for truth is evident in the reality of the classroom*

The spirituality that sheds light on educational contexts and situations enables teachers to build connections to and with learners. One of the most significant ways teachers connect with students is through their application of pedagogy. Pedagogy is understood in this case to mean the choice of methods, materials, and content employed to create effective environments where learners can successfully encounter knowledge. Pedagogy is replete with opportunities to demonstrate attitudes and behaviors that welcome and reverence diversity. Teachers who practice a pedagogy that is culturally responsive wish to connect with and incorporate students' cultures, values, languages, and traditions into their strategies for teaching content in all fields. Teachers who consistently infuse cultural concepts into the daily curriculum are able to validate in various ways the backgrounds of the learners, while simultaneously setting the stage where learners themselves can work from the complexity of their backgrounds to connect to the equally complex knowledge, attitudes, and skills needed for life at this turn of the century.

Teachers who choose culturally responsive pedagogy (CRP) over other options are interested in developing a multicultural perspective that will support their commitment to pursue options that celebrate the heritage of their students.

Why Culturally Responsive Pedagogy?

The preceding paragraphs outlined the potential benefits of such a practice. What follows is a brief background of my own introduction to CRP, a term that deserves to be understood for its potential learning benefit for all students and teachers. When I first heard about it I thought it was more educational jargon. As I investigated its nature, I began to realize that this term implies techniques for a renewed understanding of the process of education, the nature of learning, and of learners. It serves as a springboard for thinking differently about the what, how, and why of the connections teachers create with their students. CRP enhances the capacity of teachers and students.

I first heard the term culturally responsive, or relevant, pedagogy used and explained by Jacqueline Jordan Irvine at the 1997 conference of the American Association of Colleges for Teacher Education. It names the framework that guides teachers' efforts to enable children to connect what they learn in the classrooms with what they live outside of it. When such connections can be made, the process of learning is said to be relevant. This means that it sheds the light of understanding on some aspect of the learner's reality. It also means that this reality can serve as an entry point into new understandings about the world–its citizens and its potential.

At first glance this pedagogy didn't seem very different from what I would ordinarily expect. Its strategy followed excellent pedagogical tenets. Its expectations required teachers to have a thorough knowledge of the subject matter and well-developed pedagogical skills. Isn't this what is expected of every teacher? Isn't this what is known about teachers in effective schools? Even novice teachers know that effective teachers use what is known about the most effective curriculum and pedagogical practices. I found myself wondering what the difference was. If all teachers do this, what's the problem? It was really my faith in the professional integrity of Irvine, with whom I had several stimulating and challenging conversations, that made me continue to uncover the potential in this pedagogical framework.

An Inclusive Curriculum

I soon realized that this paradigm did indeed represent a renewed understanding of the firmest pedagogical principles but with a twist. It called for the generation of multiple representations, metaphors, and connections that would be built to scaffold between the learners' backgrounds and the subject matter under study (Irvine, 1997). Not only does it call the teacher forth to generate these contributions, it also calls forth similar contributions from the learners and their families. They become partners in education by contributing from their own experiences. They share their contexts and situations, their neighborhoods and their backgrounds. It may seem that such a specification is to be presumed, and maybe it is, but this paradigm calls for an authentic engagement with the familiar of the learners, their primary language, country of origin, family traditions. The neighborhood is no longer the environment that is bypassed for some more ideal concept. It becomes the testing ground for ideas, analysis, and decision-making. Speaking a language other than English is considered to be an enhancement rather than a distraction.

CRP aims to incorporate into the curriculum the contributions of people from diverse cultures and races and to add these to the scientific, literary, artistic, mathematical, and philosophical thought. It brings an honesty to instruction through a natural acknowledgment of these contributions as they are being studied. It implies the incompleteness of the canon that has formed the knowledge base for western education, and broadens it beyond Europe to include Africa and Asia. It includes the plural voices of diversity.

An Antidote To Disempowerment

Is it necessary to incorporate multiple perspectives in the curriculum? I think so and the reason becomes clear through anecdote.[1] A young girl, Taneika, proudly displayed the family picture she drew. Although Taneika and her family were black, the family she drew was white. Other details in the picture, the family car, home, and surroundings did not in the least resemble Taneika's actual life or family. Apparently she did not see herself

---

[1] This anecdote is modeled after a similar one that is recounted in the article by Patricia Goldblatt (1999).

in the process of learning. She was not an active constructor of her knowledge. What type of representations were displayed in the classroom to depict family life? What was the nature of the discussions about family that they did not include her reality? Or did they? Was her own background acknowledged? Or did she find another reality more desirable than her own? Whatever the situation, she did not situate herself within the context but projected her learning outward—toward another reality. Delpit would call this a disempowering situation (1988).

In disempowering situations the learner is distanced from the learning which is frequently bound to an external voice of authority represented by the teacher or the text. In such situations and over time learning can become an objective accumulation of elements, details, and operations—something like a pile of possessions that surround us but don't necessarily enhance our lives. At first glace, Taneika didn't achieve any understandings about the things in her environment. However, this may not be the case. Her response could indicate that the task represented not her reality but that of the dominant influence in the learning context. She might have demonstrated that she had learned compliance behaviors very well. On the other hand, her response could also signal her understanding that her reality is not acceptable or is only a temporary reality that must be shed for something better. Perhaps her young wisdom senses that it is best not to invest too much in her reality as it is but in what it might become. Certainly, any of these interpretations are possible.

Toward Empowerment
The challenge is to adjust the learning context so that the young Taneikas of our schools hear the message that they, their families, their heritage language, culture and traditions, and their neighborhoods are valued. This can be accomplished in various ways but will only happen when Taneika's teachers commit to making the choices necessary to let it happen. Cummins (1986) posits that minority students will succeed educationally to the extent that schools indicate a reverence for the backgrounds of learners. I agree and I want the same reverence to be extended to all learners.

We have perhaps all been exposed to learning experiences and aspects of life that either did not touch us or were insufficiently enticing to compel us to invest energies in them. The distancing itself is not as crucial as are its possible effects, namely alienation or demoralization. These effects might lay dormant until a later age when Taneika will be capable of reflecting on them. Or they might remain submerged and heaped upon her up to her teenage years when they burst forth with a vehemence that takes her teachers by surprise.

Engagement in learning. Alienation and demoralization represent undesirable attributes for learners. They are the diametrical opposites of engagement and enthusiasm. They exist at all grade levels and characterize some learners from all cultures, races, and socioeconomic levels. Their contexts and situations may differ but their facades are easily recognized. Teachers are bewildered and rendered powerless when faced with attitudes and behaviors that appear to be impenetrable to concerned adults. An unwritten rule known by all students tells them that when threatened by some aspect of the learning environment or society at large, they must seek refuge in isolation or surround themselves with a blanket of support from peers.

Such behavior occurs across all strata of society. It is sometimes erroneously thought that it doesn't happen in the suburbs or among learners who represent the dominant culture. It does. At one time it was considered to be a marked characteristic of adolescence. Now it appears in younger children too. Its primary link is not to age, race, and socioeconomic levels but to the learners' sense of efficacy during periods of fragile emotional development. When discussing this idea with novice-teachers, it becomes clear that the consequences of these withdrawals differ in severity according to the background of the learners. Those from wealthy backgrounds can get back on track rather quickly; while those from backgrounds that are not as privileged are faced with unsurmountable obstacles. A parallel can be drawn between a healthy individual who sustains an injury and a sickly person whose health is generally poor. The healthy person has the potential for full recovery, while the sickly person languishes and sometimes loses ground because of poor health. Just as one needs to understand that prevention is better than cure in situations where the person is healthy so too should it be for the learning process. Preventing alienation and demoralization is more desirable than having to remedy their effects.

Faced with these conditions and without the spiritual strength that comes from self-awareness and the support of a multicultural perspective, teachers themselves can become demoralized and alienated. These attitudes manifest themselves through controlling behaviors that inhibit the creation of connections. When teachers use controlling behaviors to shield themselves from the hurt and insecurity that pervade an atmosphere replete with alienation and demoralization, they appear to be detached and aloof. They seem to be unconcerned about the learners and not willing to invest any energy in forming connections with them. Rifts widen, animosity builds, trust is lost, and hope is gone.

Or so it seems. For most students hope is not gone. Many students never get to such an advanced state of alienation and demoralization; they simply act that way because it is the cool thing to do. It fits the popular slogan that proclaims the "bigger the act the badder they are!"

Although it may seem impossible, teachers are well positioned to break through these facades, or prevent alienation and demoralization altogether. The challenge of doing this is probably in proportion to the complexity of these conditions, making this task into a difficult and long-term undertaking. These conditions are not as easily reversed as the media would have us believe. Movies portray only superficially the stories of teachers who were able to connect to learners through the transformation required to overcome such conditions. The contexts in which this challenge resides are multifaceted. They look different according to societal and economic factors. Yet, despite these variations, teachers and learners face similar challenges in the inner city, in suburbia, and in rural America, in the well-equipped schools of the wealthy and in poorly equipped schools of the less wealthy. These differences notwithstanding, teachers who successfully reversed alienation and demoralization did so by creating experiences in which the learning was owned by the learners. It got inside their skin, sometimes catching them unaware and holding them until they could resist no more.

The effects just described speak of a transformation that emerges from within. Up to now, I have been focusing on a spirituality that supports a multicultural perspective, which in turn strengthens respectful connections between teachers and learners. I situated this experience within the context of education and for the sake of the teachers' mission. Now I want to suggest that when learners develop awareness of their own spirituality, they too will be strengthened and become able to connect with adults and other learners, relating with each other, taking initiative for the pursuit of learning and assuming responsibility for their attitudes and behaviors.

The Responsive Community
I suggest that this will happen within the context of an inclusive learning community that invites participation of all partners in education. It will happen when this collective community ponders the content and experiences that accurately represent multiple contributions, realities, and perspectives, and when these elements are represented in authentic ways that compel participants to encounter and make sense of their complex environments. Authenticity is a quality that emerges when learners are engaged in applying and judging knowledge and skills in relevant situations and contexts. Relevant situations and contexts are those that surround learners yet can be infused into the curriculum by way of examples and representations, applications and analysis, problem-solving, and by envisioning the future. Is there any question that such activities are part of an integrative curriculum that fosters the development of critical thinking? Is there any doubt that what learners experience today represents experiences similarly experienced by youth in the past? Is there any doubt that our first step into the future is the one we take today?

These experiences might occur in or out of schools. They may not rely on the content in textbooks. Educators who search for situations and contexts that afford students diverse opportunities to master the content standards are empowering learners to make better sense of the learning and also about the contexts and situations of their lives. The motivation for learning is sustained by a dynamic that balances internal direction with external influences and by a sense of efficacy that convinces learners of their potential, in spite of societal attitudes that might convey alternative messages. Learners who are empowered in such a way find that the empowerment serves as both a motivator and a result. Rather than find themselves in the cycle of failure, they find themselves in the cycle of success, a success that is marked by effective achievement and accomplishment. Pedagogy that fosters such a practice is culturally responsive, capacity-enhancing, and empowering.

Capacity-enhancing experiences are probably similar to peak experiences that enliven us because they tap into our innermost resources and call forth our best response. The careful creation of a classroom culture is a capacity-enhancing experience. So are learning activities that are distinguished by the type of engagement they engender, engagements that represent partnership with other learners and ownership of the learning. They yield a sense of satisfaction and they allow the learners to join their voices with those of others and make a judgment as to satisfactory authorship, authenticity, and completion.

The Imperative To Change
As I write this I am conscious that many generations of children who were successfully educated in American schools did not see themselves represented in textbooks, pictures, and other materials used by teachers in classrooms. Acknowledging this factor might be sufficient to undercut any argument in support of a pedagogy that incorporates the cultural traditions and reality of learners. Readers might wonder why such a need seems to have evolved so suddenly. Indeed, just the other day I heard a radio commentator ask rhetorically, "What happened?" He was one of seventy children in one elementary school class and yet they learned. Why do children need special programs? Why can't they learn English as immigrant children did when this commentator was in school? Times, people, education, and society have changed radically, but the change has not been so sudden. Life causes change.

Yet, these considerations are essential if teachers are to reform their educational practices. Teachers must reform them as they make decisions about the degrees of relevance they want to add to learning experiences. This will clarify the lens through which teachers comprehend how the lived experiences of learners enhance or hinder their learning. Teachers will also catch a glimpse of their own dispositions toward the students they teach. Do they teach from an ethnocentric perspective, which narrowly defines life's parameters according to their own background? Or is their perspective broad? These personal preferences represent contradictions that require a choice. The choice makes a difference in how effectively teachers will be able to connect with learners. And the choice requires change.

No one who has lived through the societal, economic, and technological revolutions of the past thirty years can deny that the way we live life as a society has changed significantly. Yet, the way we pursue education has changed neither as radically nor as rapidly. Novice teachers have grown up with the changes. They know no other experience except vicariously through stories told by previous generations. And it is well known that what happened before one's birth is really irrelevant in the life of a young person. What they do know, what they have learned through more than sixteen years' experience is how education is carried out. Their experiences of schooling are strongly imprinted on every fiber of their being and form the paradigm, or model, out of which they carry on the process of education. This does not mean that no one initiates change. Change does occur, but very slowly. My more cynical thoughts lead to describe schooling as a long course in conformity.

Young adults make independent decisions about many aspects of life, including marriage, child-bearing and rearing, leisure, and socializing. For some reason the initiative that fosters independent decisions in these personal spheres doesn't transfer into the professional sphere.

This doesn't mean that novice teachers do not think about more effective ways to carry on the educational process. My own lens was clarified during a recent conversation with some novice teachers. We were sharing cultural autobiographies, and I was transfixed by the variety of backgrounds these teachers experienced. All had been raised and educated in suburban counties outside of New York City, where high standards for educational achievement were expected. With this knowledge in mind, I presumed that they shared similar backgrounds. This is a very common error, one that I should not make. I know that geographic proximity, similar educational experiences, and common language and race do not guarantee homogeneity. Indeed, the backgrounds of these teachers were quite varied.

One teacher, Laura, told of being raised in a Polish neighborhood populated with immigrant people. She spoke Polish at home as well as around the neighborhood. When she was about seven years old her family moved to the suburbs. The ethnic neighborhood of the city gave way to the generic culture of the suburbs. It was culture not without norms and expectations, an almost unspecified culture in which she was considered different. She recalled that she spoke English with a slight accent and that her vocabulary was interspersed with Polish terms. Family traditions, names of household items, terms of endearment, and other terms that were used on a regular basis in her old neighborhood became the objects of laughter and ridicule by classmates in her new school. To add to her sense of not fitting in her teachers expected her to use standard English. She learned what many students learned before her, namely that home is home and school is school and that the two should never meet. The rich language and culture she brought with her to school were not allowed to surface. Laura recovered from this experience but remembers questioning the value of her home language and the family traditions that had provided her with a sense of security and belonging up to that time of disruption in her young life (Romeo, 2000).

Laura's teachers might have used words from her heritage language to introduce the idea that language is enriched by contributions from other tongues. After all, the study of words is an essential part of the language arts curriculum. Studying Latin's roots, its prefixes and suffixes, and its grammatical structure is acknowledged as a way to enhance performance on standardized tests. New words associated with foods of diverse cultural groups are added to our lexicon on a regular basis. Language is dynamic, and the English language has changed over time with the addition of words from various linguistic traditions. Yet, we seem to be afraid to celebrate the language that learners bring to school.

The literature about multicultural education and personal experiences in multicultural contexts tell me that our society is quite myopic. The canon of knowledge and understandings passed from one generation to the next represents the experiences of a partial group of learners. It gives lip service to those on the periphery and totally ignores those of many others. This fact has been the subject of numerous articles and books written over the past thirty-five years that have challenged these cultural boundaries as the peripheral and ignored voices emerged from their silence.

Teachers as agents of change. These voices emerged with a vehemence that gives evidence of their awareness of having been silenced for too long. They include voices of people of color, of women, of teachers. They represent alternate perspectives. They are the voices that need to be legitimized or validated by others in order to be heard.

Teachers whose voices have called out in favor of reform have gone unheeded, a difficult truth to accept. Teachers who have given their voices over to union representation frequently say, "I'd like to stay but the union says I can't." Why is it that the suggestions, issues, or ideas raised by these teachers have remained unheard? Perhaps when the voices stopped it was misinterpreted as being an indication of satisfaction rather than of abdication, of having given up and given in, or an acknowledgment that the problem never existed, that, once the concept was aired, it could be boxed without any analysis or resolution.

Teachers, acknowledging that their voices have been silenced, can reflect on whether they too silence the voices of the learners and of their parents. Such silence should not be interpreted as relating to the quiet or silence that is present during learning or studying. This kind of quiet is an acceptable condition. The quiet of learning is frequently replete with conversations that engage voices to clarify, discuss, and challenge ideas.

The silenced voices, on the other hand, speak through an atmosphere that is palpable with apathy, resentment, and alienation. That such responses surface when the wisdom of the whole group is ignored should not be surprising, yet it frequently takes teachers by surprise. I don't believe that teachers intend to create such situations. Sometimes they do so unwittingly. Sometimes the background of the learners influences their behaviors and attitudes to the extent that they carry over from one class or year to another and don't give a situation a chance.

When I speak with teachers about their concerns with regard to teaching diverse student populations, they frequently mention being insufficiently knowledgeable about and of feeling less comfortable with other people's cultures. They fear that their actions will be misinterpreted because of unfamiliarity with cultural patterns. They are concerned that careless speech exchange among learners will be hurtful and are insufficiently confident to address it. They perceive a lack of trust, a lack of motivation, and the subsequent can't do it mind-set. They recognize that their own lack of exposure to diverse populations leaves them underprepared to interact effectively with parents who may hold different views, ideals, and values. They are concerned about their ability to balance instruction while accommodating different learning styles. They are concerned about being effective teachers to learners whose strongest language is not English. They are concerned about reaching all learners to help them develop and enhance their capacities.

These concerns are authentic and they must be addressed honestly through reflection to determine whether they are a regular part of interpersonal interactions and trends in society or whether they are compounded by issues of diversity or inclusion. Some concerns can surface in schools where teachers feel at one with the population, for example a suburban-born and educated teacher in a suburban school, or an urban-born and educated teacher in an urban school. Compatibility might be felt in places with similar socioeconomic levels or religion, or habits of interpersonal relationships and expectations. When one or more of these variables are encountered in a culturally diverse context, their impact is perceived to be greater, even threatening. I suppose the greater the diversity with relation to language, race, and neighborhood, the greater the perceived threat. The threat compounded when multiple variables cross.

While the perception of sameness may permit us to enter a context or situation gracefully, the presumption of sameness may give us a false sense of security. If we assume that those who look like us are like us, we may very quickly confront a reality that catches us unaware. As we scratch the surface of our lives we realize the multiple perspectives that reside in each of us. We discover our uniqueness, idiosyncracies, and peculiarities which exist because we are different. The essential understanding that emerges from reflection and probing into these differences reveals that this difference signifies neither lack of validity nor correctness but, in fact, our common humanity.

If we work through the complexities and paradoxes of our differences, and if we choose to do so with our students, we begin to find that place where conversation about differences can safely occur. We can allow understanding to emerge through greater awareness of the contributions brought by each person. As we acknowledge and probe our common humanity we can structure the culture of the classroom.

Within a classroom culture, a community of learners can grow while simultaneously defining the individuality of its members. Futrell and Witty (1997) define culture as the confluence of language, beliefs, values, traditions, and behaviors that permeate our lives (p. 191). If this is true of the larger society, is it not also true of the culture of the classroom? Culture can be thoughtfully developed when it is allowed to emerge from the diversity of the members. We are not slaves to our culture, we create it through thoughtful decisions about the type of interactions that occur in classrooms.

I believe that CRP provides the appropriate guidelines for developing a classroom culture that is capacity enhancing. The time is ripe for us to move forward in creating a reality from a vision of education that is more compatible with the cultural diversity of our students.

Moving Teachers into CRP

This action-research project asks teachers to analyze an existing lesson for cultural relevance which is demonstrated through outcomes, materials, learning activities, and potential application of what is learned. This project achieves what it is designed to accomplish. Teachers are surprised that changes to their plans can be made with relative ease primarily because they are focused on cultural learnings. They are amazed at the observable change in learners' motivation and the consequent enhanced achievement of content standards. Sample lessons and reflections taken from in-class writing and formal projects are presented below.

How Teachers Respond to the Challenge of CRP

Focusing on cultural values. Martin McCabe (2000), realized the immeasurable potential that literature has for teaching about cultures and traditions. In his original lesson, he used the story *The Rough-Face Girl* to introduce fourth graders to various aspects of the life style of American Indians. He also wanted the students to compare this folktale with the familiar Cinderella story. In reflecting on the original lesson, he became aware of broader possible applications and he revised his plan accordingly.

McCabe realized the potential to learn much more about Native American people from this story than their housing and survival skills. One major lesson revolves around the strong theme of natural and inner beauty, in contrast to the external beauty of the princess found in the popular American Cinderella story. In *The Rough-Face Girl*, the oppressed sister is not transformed into a beautiful princess whose beauty captures the prince's love. *The Rough-Face Girl* captures the desired man's love through her simplicity, love of nature, and pure, kind heart. The invisible being (or man) does not acknowledge the scared or ragged appearance of the girl. He initially falls in love with her gentleness and respect for nature, both cherished values of American Indians.

In revising the outcomes for his plan, the teacher, McCabe, focused on the values of the American Indians rather than on the physical aspects of their villages and their lifestyle, which formed the focus of the original lesson. He maintained the activity that investigated similarities and differences between the two versions of the Cinderella story. He also added an activity that compared the values portrayed in the story of the rough-face girl with the values of the American Indian nations as they are understood today.

In his final comments, McCabe acknowledged how shifting the focus of the lesson toward beliefs and values opened the potential to expand the study of cultures through the traditional tales of the people.

Infusing multicultural principles. The experience of reflecting on CRP led another teacher, Currivan (2000), to reconsider the criteria she used to measure successful teaching and learning in a unit on *The Catcher in the Rye*. Currivan's reflections yielded the awareness that while the lessons she planned were politically correct, they were lacking in any cultural outcomes. Through reflection, she acknowledged that only some—but not all—students understood that Holden Caufield's identity struggle was similar to their own. She assumed everyone was learning, even though the remarks of some students indicated otherwise.

In reviewing her lessons in light of the criteria for CRP, Currivan did not change the learning outcomes. Rather, she shifted the focus of the discussion away from Caufield's sense of isolation and toward the personal struggles that students experienced. She asked students to consider how their family traditions, cultural values, gender, sexual identity, and achievement influenced their struggles. Out of this discussion they constructed an *everyteen* prototype. She then presented tales of identity crises from other cultural and racial perspectives and asked the students to compare these with their own. Finally, she directed the students to include Caufield's character in the comparisons they were discussing.

While observing the students participate in the revised lesson, Currivan came to the startling observation that this was the first time ever that the class was truly united. She credits the obvious solidarity to the intense interest in and appreciation of the diverse backgrounds. As the students conferred with each other, their discussion about *teenness* took on a sophistication that was not apparent prior to this experience. All were involved in contributing something concrete from their personal experiences and in listening respectfully to each other. Currivan felt herself fade into the background as the students engaged in a journey toward self-discovery, which replaced the less effective psychological character analysis of her original lesson.

Inviting parents' input. Sometimes teachers think that their social studies classes are inherently multicultural. One high school social studies teacher claimed that she was not sure she could rework her already culturally responsive lesson according to the tenets of CRP. However, in true spirit of openness she selected a lesson that is part of a unit on the Vietnam War, and she decided to focus on a small group of students representing a great deal of diversity.

Using as an opener a documentary that presents letters from soldiers fighting in Vietnam, Wright (2000) would follow up by asking students to read excerpts from texts of presidential actions and speeches. After the readings, the students were to write a summary of the major events of the Vietnam War.

In revising the lesson, Wright took advantage of the diverse backgrounds represented by the students in her class. The parents of some of these students had immigrated from Asia, Europe, and South America, although the majority was born in the United States. The religious backgrounds of the families were as diverse as were the political perspectives, which seemed to span the full spectrum from liberal to conservative. Students were directed to interview their families about their personal experiences during the Vietnam War. They were also asked to summarize their interviews in their journals. Although some students protested and complained about having to do this assignment, they all complied.

Wright reported several outcomes of her efforts to revise the lesson. One was the value of the personalized understandings from family-based dialogues that students had never gleaned from reading the primary and secondary sources alone. Another was the opportunity to converse about the Vietnam War with two fathers who called her, one to express his appreciation that his experiences were considered sufficiently valuable to be included in his daughter's education, and another to thank her for providing a rare opportunity to have a significant, adult-like conversation with his son. Another outcome benefited a student who knew very little about his father who fought in Vietnam and suffered terribly in its aftermath. Another student learned that her parents had little knowledge of the Vietnam War because they were too concerned about political persecution in their own native land. Yet another student learned about the involvement in the war of a country that was previously thought to have been uninvolved.

This foray into CRP has convinced Wright of its effectiveness. She is planning to repeat this revised lesson with larger classes during the next school year. Her eyes are now open to the possibilities for social studies instruction to expand on the basic knowledge contained in textual material.

Acknowledging countries of origin. Several years ago, a novice teacher planned a lesson on the meaning of flags. One activity required every child to draw the flag of the United States. Given the opportunity to reconsider the plan according to the criteria for CRP, she realized that had the children been asked to research and to draw the flag of the countries from which their families had immigrated, they would have achieved authentic cultural learnings.

Although she knew that the students had learned accurate content in the original lesson, she understood that the revised lesson would have broadened their multicultural perspective. Her additional comment that both her cooperating teacher and her supervisor were as ignorant of CRP as she was well taken. Each had rated her lesson as excellent and offered no suggestions for change.

Studying native foods. Science teacher Fernandez-Cabrera (2000) wanted her lessons to incorporate as much diversity as her students represented. After reviewing a unit on nutrition, she revised the questions that she used to call forth students' prior knowledge. In previous years, she had asked students to analyze the nutrition facts printed on cereal boxes, although she knew that most of her students didn't eat cereal for breakfast. They ate traditional breakfasts of bread and coffee.

In the revised plan, she asked students to list their favorite foods from their culture, analyze their nutritional values, and research where these foods came from. She also assigned students to research the contributions of an African American food chemist and to investigate common diseases associated with their culture's nutrition. In reflecting on the different responses elicited by the revised lesson, Fernandez-Cabrera realized that incorporating multiple perspectives helped learners to develop alternative explanations and world views.

These examples demonstrate how small changes can intensify cultural learning. They also open the door to another consideration about the qualitative aspects of teaching and learning. As so often happens when innovative ideas are presented, questions arise about the practices these ideas are meant to replace. Some questions refer to the validity or correctness of the older practices, while others cause teachers to ask if they've made wrong choices in the past.

Transformed Pedagogy Equals Transformed Teachers

I believe that the most effective professional transformations arise from a sense of humility that helps all people realize that they are neither all-wise nor all-knowing. By its nature, professionalism prompts teachers to teach authentic content through practices that are considered most effective. Professionalism also leads teachers toward self-renewal as they read professional literature, attend conferences, and confer with colleagues. These activities will inform further development of their repertoire of methodologies and techniques. Teachers are decision makers. They must choose from many options the ones they believe will lead their students toward multicultural perspectives that will enable them to live effectively in this culturally diverse society. If CRP provides a framework for doing just that, professional teachers will choose to follow its guidelines.

I will end this chapter with the sentiments expressed by an experienced teacher who responded enthusiastically to CRP. May (1998) linked this pedagogy with her growing awareness about listening to multiple voices, including those of learners. At one time in her teaching career she thought that she needed to say the right thing at all times. She thought that the teacher should refrain from stating her opinion on what was being learned. As she delved into CRP, she began to realize that the crux of the problem was that too frequently the teacher's opinion is the only one heard. Just as frequently, what is said emanates from ethnocentric textbooks. She summarized her revised vision by acknowledging that as time passes and she becomes more familiar with new ways of thinking, her ability to scan different perspectives and keep an open mind to everyday problems and challenges will increase.

Chapter Nine
Envisioning the Future

Teachers who recreate their classroom practices and enhance the interpersonal relationships between and among students do so not only for the benefit of the current student population but also with an eye to the future. Today's students are tomorrow's leaders. If there is but one idea that needs to be implanted in their minds, it is that they can create their future, preferably a future that is without violence. I open this chapter with a report of a discussion about violence that was initiated by a teacher one evening during class. Following this report I describe a technique that can be used to dream about the future we desire and to learn how to work toward actualizing it. Belief in the future in an essential human endeavor.

An Unusual Question

Perhaps you can imagine my surprise recently when a teacher asked whether violence wasn't an essential element of life. According to the young man who asked the question, life without violence would be boring. It would have no challenge. Life without violence would lack the motivation to be alert to the dangers of the environment. Honestly, such thoughts had never crossed my mind. Having lived during times when violence was less rampant than it is today, I know that life can be very enriching without it. I know that beauty and serenity can motivate people to be alert to the environment in ways that violence never can. I know that boredom results from factors other than a lack of violence. However, the reality of today is that violence pervades our lives without respect for anyone or anything. It invades personal and public spaces. Its entry into these spaces sparks reactions of disruption and damage. It is pervasive, and even with the best of intentions to avoid it, people get stuck in its grip.

Every type of media displays it; books and periodicals contain articles about it. Neither sports events nor children's games are beyond its grasp. It is built into toys. It is even experienced in other ways. Too many of the children sitting in schools today are regularly subjected to violence in the form of physical, emotional, and sexual abuse. If a disease that deadly were to spread so rampantly, massive relief efforts to curtail it would surely be enacted. Yet, violence seems to be beyond check. The realization of the extent to which violence consumes energy, diverts attention, and undermines a sense of personal safety is startling. This monolithic horror has permeated life to such an extent that it is taken for granted. Why are we so powerless against it?

Attempts to distinguish the nature, sources, and manifestations of violence reveal the extent to which it is not understood. Nevertheless, the task is essential if we are ever to contain it. I believe that the absence of an accepted understanding of such a concept does nothing to change its reality, whereas the evidence of such an understanding can provide a standard to be applied when incidents of violence are analyzed. I also believe that it is better to pursue these understandings out of personal experiences rather than research, lest discussions become overly academic.

The focus of the discussion in class that evening centered on whether violence is ever a worthy or appropriate reaction. The few answers and several questions that were raised accentuated the complexity of the issue. It soon became apparent that observable behaviors may not be effective indicators of violence, whose explosive nature is matched only by its elusiveness. Is violence a conscious act of aggression? Is its onset obvious, an inevitable outburst emanating from emotions like rage, fury, passion, wrath? Is its onset startling, hidden beneath a facade that is marked by tranquility, serenity, or composure? Is violence an inevitable component of human nature? Can it be controlled? Is it a choice among alternatives? Is it ever justified?

Why is it that seemingly random acts of violence take us by surprise? Have we been lulled into the false belief that economic security, guarded relationships with neighbors, and competition among peers guarantee safety? Do we really believe that huge houses, sophisticated alarms, gated communities, guns, knives, pepper spray, and various other weapons ensure protection? We build more prisons and reinstate the death penalty. Then we wonder why children engage in acts of violence against themselves and other children. In such a society, where trust is weak and hope is nearing abandonment, we must turn to alternative sources for answers.

Creative Alternatives

Last year I came upon a collection of poems written by Desmond Egan about the Famine in Ireland. This event of the mid-1800s was marked by brutal subjugation, pillage, persecution, and silencing of traditions and language. The famine is etched in the psyches of succeeding generations of Irish families. Much violence has been carried out in response to atrocities heaped on this small island nation, so much so that several generations of youngsters have known no other way of life. And yet, the rage felt by Egan is vented in a masterly fashion through poetry. Its power holds the potential to heal memories, to replace anger and anguish with a serenity that comes only after enormous suffering. Egan's response is nonviolent, decisively chosen from among many options. Such a response doesn't eliminate, condone, or ameliorate the violence that roused the anguish. Rather, it releases the devastating effects that well up in people who harbor feelings and thoughts of revenge in the wake of violence.

Poets like Egan are owed a debt of gratitude for they lead the way out of a maze of tangled emotions and directionless resolution. Their creative responses are inviting, drawing people together. They offer the potential for consolation and comfort in the wake of violence. They offer an alternative vision, one that models how an act of creation can lead to healing, reconciliation, and maybe even forgiveness.

While few of us are gifted with the poet's eloquence, many of us can dream. It is in the dreaming that we can do for ourselves what the poet does in writing: We can imagine the reality that we desire to create.

Creating a New Vision

I am reminded of a technique that incorporates dreams to create something anew. Called "envisioning the future," it contains moments where people can sit quietly and breathe deeply for a few minutes to clear the mind, imagine what an ideal life would be like in thirty years, dream about it for several minutes, share the dreams, and determine what needs to be done to create it. This technique can be used in groups large and small and can be adapted to many different scenarios. My purpose in using it with teachers is that they generally focus on schools and students and themselves for their dream session. As a result, they can think differently about solutions to some of the problems they face today. Violence is one of these problems.

As the sharing of the dreams ensues, people's ideas expand when they hear something they want to incorporate into their future. After the sharing, they are asked to identify benchmarks, starting in the future. Their dream becomes the goal set for the thirty-year mark. They are asked to spell out what will be in place in twenty-five years, in twenty, and so on, every five years until they come back to the present. This reverse planning helps to keep the focus on the goal.

Once the benchmarks have been set, it is necessary to consider what has to be accomplished to reach the thirty-year mark. Such thinking releases creative energy that charges the atmosphere of the room with life, enthusiasm, and hope. It transforms the participants. They look and feel different, having a renewed sense of accomplishment and a sense of efficacy. The locus of control has been firmly grasped during this exercise, and in the ensuing debriefing some very important ideas about power and control are discussed.

Control is power that can be used constructively toward empowerment of self and others, or destructively toward demoralization. Violence is an extreme form of destructive control. It is an exercise of abusive power. Delpit (1988) makes some very strong claims about power. One is that issues of power are played out through rules that reflect the culture of the dominant cultural group and that govern schools and classrooms. Another claim is that those with the most power are the least aware of how they exert it and least willing to admit it. These ideas cause much discomfort to many teachers who think of power only in the negative sense and tend to proclaim their powerlessness. Yet, the teachers who acknowledge the significant power they have access to can learn to use it effectively to transform the present and create what is desirable for the future.

Teachers need to understand that they can exert power to create classroom communities where mutuality and harmony are valued above domination and mastery. Timothy Radcliff (1999) claims that violence emerges in groups of people who have forgotten how to do things together. Teachers who value cooperation over competition can teach youngsters about ways to rely on each other. When cooperation is high, trust expands, communication opens, and hope emerges. Connections are made and violence ceases to exist.

If we return to the question that was raised initially, we can acknowledge that throughout this engaging, creative, and non-violent experience, boredom was nil, while motivation was high. People noticed the energy that charged the atmosphere. The sense of harmony that pervaded this cooperative process was combined with much laughter and enjoyment. At such times, teachers felt the boost to their spirit, and it is this spirit that continues to motivate them to pursue their mission.

Famine[1]

Took away our great forests
took our cattle away
took away our farming
our wool our linen our glass
grabbed the very plots
from under our hungry eyes
starved our language
tried our religion too
tumbled a nation's destiny
   drove us
into the ditches of Europe
and onto the sad tides

one thousand years of murder
one thousand years of plunder
one thousand years of rape
the curse of Raleigh on you
the curse of Cromwell too
one thousand years in cells
one thousand years climbing
the gallows the gibbet the wooden triangle
and the disciplined army lash
beginning at 500 strokes

the greatest blessing
ask the natives

children should be taught
   pride in
their imperial heritage its
transformation of the
   world
for the lasting benefit of
literally millions

time we gave serious
   thought to
the nobler instincts that
   drove
generations of Britons
to risk their lives building
The Empire

to make a profit
under God

---

[1] I am grateful to Desmond Egan (1997) for allowing me to print this poem in its entirety.

one thousand years
one thousand years
of war and famine and the plague
one thousand years on the run

one thousand years of dying
instead of being alive

took away our childhood
took our parents away
sisters brothers families
took away our heroes
too bitter too bitter a list
knotted our future into a past
to whip us with

gave us pax Britannica
slavery beneath the slavery
of the slaving capital of the world
gave us plenty to die for
gave us their neuroses
the nervous tics of empire
their need to be admired
and threw in as a bonus
their honest astonishment at
our refusal to be improved

the locals are what would
be understood
in England as starved
and what is understood
in Ireland as half-starved

Chapter Ten
Effective Teachers

In this culminating chapter I present my vision of an effective teacher. Following this statement of vision, I include selections from various assignments completed by teachers who are students in a graduate program

Effective teachers are characterized by two dynamic realities: They are professionals who learn as much about their students as they can, and they are effective leaders whose knowledge of their subject and personal integrity inspire a degree of confidence that moves students to accept their authority and to cooperate in the task of creating a community of learners. This personal statement is how I envision teachers. It situates the teaching-learning process in an interpersonal as well as intrapersonal context in which learning is expected to occur. It is an outgrowth of reflection prompted by Sarason (1993) and of subsequent interviews with many preservice teachers who were asked to describe their most successful learning experiences.

The experiences described being totally involved with reading, discussing, practicing, analyzing, synthesizing, and evaluating tasks, ideas and issues. They recalled being challenged by the complexity of the task, and although at times their confidence wavered they knew they would succeed. All mentioned that a particularly caring teacher believed in them and supported their efforts. Common descriptors of successful learning that I have gleaned during these interviews over ten years included involvement, challenge, and support by a teacher who became significant because of the quality of the interaction. Differences mentioned included the place of the learning, its focus, and the age or grade of the learner, which went from the age of eight through the college degree. An additional difference was in the learners' perception of being successful. While many relied on prior successful learning experiences, just as many indicated that they did not perceive themselves to be smart. They were convinced that they were incapable of succeeding when faced with a challenging task and preferred to avoid facing it. These learners credited their willingness to attempt a challenging task to the faith that the teacher had in them. They credited their ability to stay with it to its completion to the teacher's ongoing support.

This group also claimed that the self-esteem that resulted from their experience supported them through actual experiences, in other contexts, and with different teachers. It is out of these descriptors that the following description of effective teachers emanates.

Effective Teachers as Described by Their Students

Effective teachers are professionals who learn as much about their students as they can. Effective teachers are learners who have successfully struggled with complexity themselves, and are predisposed to sustain efforts to broaden their content and pedagogical knowledge in order to discover effective ways to connect students and content. Effective teachers strive to motivate students to accept their authority and to participate in the task of creating a learning community.

How do teachers grow into such a description? Of course, after reading this book, readers might believe that they have been set up for the obvious response, and I would agree. I suggest that teachers who acknowledge their cultural influences and develop their spirituality through reflection are inclined to consider the needs of a culturally diverse population. They are more accepting of a diversity of opinion, values, behaviors and are, therefore, more positively disposed to developing a multicultural perspective. This perspective encourages them to build their teaching around authentic and significant cultural understanding, and to incorporate the families and neighborhoods of learners. These teachers learn about the students whose lives they touch on a daily basis and perhaps for all time.

When teachers are asked their opinions about these ideas, their responses are varied, interesting, and informational. Some teachers doubt that they have any culture or spirituality but willingly engage in the reflective investigation to see what awaits their discovery. Usually they discover a spirituality and a culture that they took for granted. Just as the ability to walk or to enjoy good health comes into scrutiny only when impinged by some undeniable factor, so do spirituality and culture, but with a slight difference. The physical aspects of our being are quite obvious. We know when something is askew and we seek medical treatment. Intangibles such as culture or spirituality are impacted regularly during interactions with others, but without attention they remain elusive and somewhat ambiguous. The process of reflection provides a framework through which they can be understood for what they are and for how they can help teachers connect with themselves and with the culturally diverse population of learners and their parents.

Some teachers know intuitively that reflection helps them to be sensitive to learners' cultural and religious traditions. They report that it helps them to be alert to factors in contexts and situations that they might otherwise dismiss or bypass as being unimportant. Phrases such as, "I just never thought about it" or "I'm amazed" express the surprised reactions that some teachers have to the processes described in this book. These processes focus on reflection and enable the consideration of alternative viewpoints.

Some teachers acknowledge the spirituality at the core of their being, which dictates how they relate to students. They claim that their spirituality helps them to accept change in themselves and in others and to maintain a positive attitude. The changes that occur and the outlooks that develop surprise and delight them. Most often they report that they now think more deeply and objectively about something before commenting on it. Their comments also change as they are informed by the multiple perspectives brought to the analysis. In turn, interactions between teachers and students become more confident, effective, and healing. Teachers who foster their spirituality feel freer to accept others because they are more accepting of themselves.

Others aren't convinced that they would describe the inner prompting toward transformation as spirituality. Yet they do admit that they become transformed through reflection and critical analysis of the context and situations associated with teaching. Some teachers prefer the term open-mindedness. The term that describes this central disposition is secondary to the process and the results it yields.

One teacher commented that the students and their parents need to be as spiritual as the teacher in order to be fulfilled and enriched by the learning. Another acknowledges that the connection students make to the learning process must reside beyond cognition, in some deeper and less tangible place.

Teachers in general are amazed to discover the similarities among the diverse cultures their students bring to the classroom and their own too. When they tune in to the diversity of the students, they realize the amount of rejoicing that occurs around this diversity and count this among the spiritual dimensions of teaching. It is from such a realization that one teacher claims her spirituality brings a calm peace that remains with her even when tested. Another teacher reported her amazement that feelings she thought were buried deeply in her psyche could be changed after such a long time.

The unexamined beliefs held by teachers are fertile fields for reflection. Beliefs are the deepest, most sacred values held by humans. Teachers' beliefs relate to their views of culturally diverse learners and their families, how learning occurs, the pedagogy they choose to practice, the accommodations they pursue for students with special needs, and their dispositions toward life-long learning. These beliefs are expressed in philosophy that represents the wisdom that they have come to love.

Teachers Express Their Beliefs

The philosophy of multicultural education is a project of action and reflection through which teachers express the beliefs that guide their teaching practices. A fuller development of this reflection occurs when teachers can explain why they think as they do and also identify examples of practices that demonstrate congruence between what they profess and what they do. Teachers are surprised by the challenge of such a task. As they work to achieve clarity of expression, they are amazed at the transformation that occurs in how they think about what they do. The products that result from this process take various forms, three of which are presented here.

Middle-school teacher Bill Rolon, who works with a vastly diverse student population, articulated his personal beliefs about multicultural education in an essay he wrote while completing his master's degree. Rolon's (2000, p. 5) beliefs are summarized in the following text:

> I believe that Multicultural education respects diversity. It emphasizes the contributions of the various groups that make up the population of the world. It emphasizes the importance of people sharing their stories and learning the stories of others.
> I believe that Multicultural education respects individuality while promoting respect for others. It acknowledges that children have different learning styles and encourages teachers to search for connections between the learner and the material for academic success.
> I believe that Multicultural education produces socially active, critically thinking members of this democratic society. It encourages critical analysis of material presented in the classroom and extends this analysis to what students encounter outside of the classroom.
> I believe that Multicultural education makes all of us part of history by focusing on real issues. I believe that Multicultural education helps students make sense out of their everyday life.

The inherent potential in the last statement that Rolon offers is in keeping with the thesis of this book, namely, that spirituality is associated with people who reflect on contexts and situations in order to make sense of them. To think that one's inherent beliefs might foster a cyclical or a trickle-down effect of spirituality is most appropriate. It has long been known that students learn as much, if not more, from teachers' attitudes and behaviors than they do from their words.

Currivan (2000) opens the essay containing her belief statements by commenting that "it should be unnecessary to talk about multicultural education." However, she recognizes that need, which stems from various influences—including the media's flaunting of individuality, and rivalries between and among groups who want to sell products and services. She recommends that we revel in our individuality while striving for solidarity. It is not surprising, therefore, that her statements express respect and recognition of potential differences. She identifies four beliefs.

The first is that people are indeed different. While these differences are often culturally based, they may also be based on alternative life styles and other preferences and orientations. Everyone has a claim to a cultural background whose roots are valuable, interesting, and important to personal identity.

Currivan's second tenet, an extension of the first, proclaims that all of the representations of humanity are entitled to equal recognition and respect. Discrimination seems to escalate in spite of massive efforts by organizations to prevent it. Yet teachers are held legally responsible for the safety and equality of all members of the educational community. How times have changed! Thirty years ago teachers encouraged children to include everyone in their games. Now teachers must protect the broader perspectives of diversity, including sexual orientation, religion, gender, and race. These are common civil rights, but conflicting opinions exist regarding the appropriateness of discussing these rights and correcting behaviors that violate them. Teachers are privy to only a few blatant violations of these rights, which occur during school hours, but many children suffer from cruel treatment that remains obscure. Currivan acknowledges the fine line that teachers must walk and their vulnerability as they walk it.

Her third tenet is that successful resolution of bias-related conflict depends on effective communication. Communication may take different forms but it must always be respectful and be built on thoughtful listening. This type of listening is focused on what the speaker is expressing not what the listener thinks the speaker is expressing. Speakers must refrain from blurting out hurtful and judgmental remarks that can escalate into full-blown conflicts before a teacher can intervene.

Finally, Currivan states that teachers must rigorously examine curriculum and align pedagogy in a culturally responsive manner. Included in cultural responsiveness are the resources of the community and the families representing diverse cultural backgrounds and traditions. These efforts are expended not only toward the more effective learning of the curriculum but also toward the validation of diverse cultures. Efforts that foster a cohesive learning community will yield a sense of inclusion that is based on knowledge and respect. It will forestall the foment that encourages groups to splinter off because of fear, distrust, and ignorance of the traditions of others. Ultimately, it will forestall the eruption of violence that is the result of feelings of exclusion.

The following belief statements are excerpted from Wright's (2000) statement of multicultural philosophy. She believes that it is essential for students to understand their own culture and its role in the formation of their personal belief systems before they can begin to appreciate and understand the culture and beliefs of others. She also says that there is a clear dynamic power in classrooms and schools in general, and that, unless handled cautiously and fairly, it can effectively dampen students' interest in learning. These beliefs move her to foster a sense of responsible citizenship in her students. Included in that sense must be a certain degree of tolerance[1] for others. Her rationale for these beliefs and actions is that, as human beings, it is essential that we learn to communicate effectively with one another if we ever hope to reach a place of mutual understanding and even appreciation.

Articulating a Philosophy of Multicultural Education

When in the course of their careers teachers set about the task of articulating their philosophy of multicultural education, they squarely encounter the complexity of their profession and their mission. They generally report feeling overwhelmed by the multitude of ideas that flood their consciousness and by the enormity of the task of organizing these. After completing the articulation, they generally have a sense of satisfaction that comes about from delving deeply into their personal beliefs. Indeed, teachers' philosophical statements should express their beliefs about those aspects surrounding them, namely, the learners, the process of education, human nature, and society.

As I understand it the word philosophy means love of wisdom. Thus it follows that pertinent questions can guide teachers in this task. What is the wisdom that I have learned to love about those aspects that surround my profession? How does this wisdom guide me in the decisions I make on a daily basis? How do my beliefs translate into the pedagogy I use? How do they guide my interpersonal interactions? How do they motivate me to

---

[1] Tolerance is a less desirable disposition that is replaced by respect and reverence as the multicultural perspective emerges.

engage in professional development activities in order to enhance my effectiveness in the classroom?

The consideration of multicultural education adds another dimension to the philosophy that is particularly challenging. It is simply insufficient to indicate that the beliefs expressed are applicable to all learners. They might be, but the imperative to awaken our consciousness to the culturally diverse population is of paramount importance as this new century gets underway.

Epilogue

This book is intended to inspire teachers to be faithful to their mission. It expects great things of teachers and I believe that the majority of people who choose to enter or to remain in this profession are capable of meeting these expectations. They are special people who want to dedicate their lives to human service. Because they are motivated by spiritual promptings to work toward the betterment of other human beings, teachers, like nurses and social workers tend to become very involved in the lives of their students. Sometimes they extend this involvement to the families and neighborhoods of these students. People whose lives are dedicated to providing human services—those who connect with others—frequently encounter burnout.

Humans have a unique capacity to be unpredictable and uncontrollable, defying the best made plans of any person who provides services to them. While this reality may stymy us, it should not take us by surprise. On the one hand, education should allow learners to define themselves and it should be expected that plans won't work out as originally intended. On the other hand, reform efforts, too many to number, have been enacted toward improved learning and have yielded disappointing results. These realities create a tension that must be balanced by teachers, administrators, and public officials—not to yield to mediocrity—but to preserve human dignity and to recognize the fragility of human effort. In light of these ideas, I end with one caution. As we continue to respond to the challenge of building connections with the culturally diverse student population, we need to be aware of the importance of nurturing ourselves. We do this in several ways, and I want to suggest that we start by being gentle with our own spirit and by taking care to nurture our bodies through healthy choices about regular exercise, proper nutrition, and sufficient rest.

Being gentle with our own spirit means to acknowledge the special contribution we make to society through our mission and to give ourselves a few vacations each day. I heard a speaker make this suggestion many years ago. At first I thought it was absurd. However, as she began to expand her thoughts, I soon began to realize its wisdom. The daily vacations she advocates are really about setting aside personal time for us alone. It might be as short as ten minutes of uninterrupted listening to music, or praying, or reflecting, or just being. It might be thirty minutes to an hour for a walk, workout, or reading. Busy people, who frequently claim that they do not have even ten minutes for themselves, have the greatest need for these vacations. Teachers who carve such time out of their busy days find that they are better able to connect with students and colleagues in ways that they deem most effective.

Teachers would do well to avoid falling for the myth of perfection. Perfection is way beyond our human capabilities, and trying to attain it is folly. It leads to too many negative self-perceptions, and it does more harm than good. Because teachers are called to accountability in such unfathomable ways, the tendency is to do everything right, to be effective and efficient, to be perfect. Be aware. Avoid confusing this tendency with the essential mission of teaching I've stated previously, that is, to touch the spirit of students and to walk with them toward self-fulfillment. This mission is a human one that invites sharing at its deepest level, connecting with others humanly and spiritually. Don't be perfect, be human!

References

Buber, M. (1970). *I-Thou*. New York: Scribner.

Clinton, H.R. (1996). *It takes a village*. New York: Simon & Schuster.

Cochran-Smith, M. (1997). Knowledge, skills, and experiences for teaching culturally diverse learners: A perspective for practicing teachers. In J.J. Irvine (Ed.), *Critical knowledge for diverse teachers and learners*. (pp 27–88). Washington, DC: AACTE.

Coles, R. (1990). *The spiritual life of children*. Boston: Houghton Mifflin.

Cummins, J. (1986). Empowering minority students: A framework for intervention. *Harvard Educational Review, 56 (1)*, 18–36

Cunningham, E. M. (1989). Sabbatical reflections. *Dominican Ashram, 8*, 172–175.

Delpit, L. (1988). The silenced dialogue: Power and pedagogy in educating other people's children. *Harvard Educational Review, 5 (8)*, 280–298.

Egan, D. (1997). *Famine*. Newbridge, Co. Kildare, Ireland: Goldsmith.

Freire, P. (1970). *Pedagogy of the oppressed*. New York: Continuum Press.

Futrell, M. H. & Witty, E. P. (1997). Preparation and professional development of teachers for culturally diverse schools: Perspectives from the standards movement. *Critical knowledge for diverse teachers and learners*. (pp. 189–216). Washington, DC: AACTE.

Giroux, H. (1994). Youth and the challenge of pedagogy. *Harvard Educational Review, 64*, 278–308.

Goldblatt, P. (1999). Using stories to introduce and teach multicultural literature. *Multicultural Review, 8 (2)*, 52–58.

Gollnick, D. M., & Chinn, P. (1998). *Multicultural education in a pluralistic society*. Englewood Cliffs, NJ: Prentice Hall.

Greer, C. (1994). Pignatelli, F. & Pflaum, S. W. (Eds.). *Experiencing diversity: Toward educational equity*. Thousand Oaks, CA: Corwin Press.

Harris, M. (1988). *Women and teaching*. New York: Paulist Press.

Irvine, J. J. (Ed.). (1997). *Critical knowledge for diverse teachers and learners*. Washington, DC: AACTE.

Kozol, J. (1991). *Savage inequalities*. New York: Crown

Küng, H. (1996). *Global responsibility*. New York: Continuum Press.

Mabry, J. R. (1995). Bede Griffiths: Holy man for our time. [Online] Available *http://www.ecsd.vom/`grace/smabry/bede.html*. March 11, 1999.

Maslow, A. H. (1968). Some educational implications of the humanistic psychologies. *Harvard Educational Review, 38*, 685–696.

Nelson, M. H. (1993). *Teacher stories*. Ann Arbor: Prakken Publishers.

O'Shea, D. (1992). *In the potter's house*. Dublin, Ireland: Dominican Publications.

Radcliff, T. (1999). *Sing a new song*. Springfield, IL: Templegate

Sarason, S. (1993). *You are thinking of teaching?* San Francisco: Jossey-Bass.

Wolfe, J. (1999). Black like me. The New York Times Magazine, 14:78.

Woods, Richard. (1998) *Mysticism and prophecy*. Maryknoll: Orbis Books.

Wurzel, J. S. (Ed.) (1988). *Toward multiculturalism*. Yarmouth, ME: Intercultural Press.

Unpublished works

Currivan, A. R. (2000). Culturally responsive pedagogy.

———. (2000). Philosophy of multicultural education.

Fernandez-Cabrera, O. (2000). Cultural autobiography.

———. (2000). Action research case study: Related to culturally responsive pedagogy.

May, M. (1998). Action research case study.

McCabe, M. (2000). Action research case study.

Rolon, B. (2000). Philosophy of multicultural education.

Romeo, L. (2000). Cultural autobiography.

Wright, K. (2000). Culturally responsive pedagogy.

———. (2000). Statement of multicultural philosophy.

Index

A
Assimilation, 54
Assumptions, 7, 31, 65, 67-72, 80, 81; analysis of, 7, 67, 68, 72
Awareness, 3, 7, 12-14, 21, 30, 31, 38-40, 45, 48, 50, 51, 57-60, 62, 64, 70, 91, 94, 96, 98, 101

B
Bias, 62, 114

C
Conflict, 11, 16, 32, 35, 36, 49, 50, 61, 62, 65, 70, 75, 77, 83, 114; cultural, 16-18; interpersonal conflict, 49, 50
Connections, xii, 2, 3, 6-11, 13-15, 17, 18, 20, 39, 40, 42-44, 56, 59, 64, 67, 72, 83, 85-87, 90, 107, 113, 117
Contemplation, 32
Critical analysis, 69, 77, 78, 111, 113

Culture, xi-xiii, 1, 12, 19, 25, 27, 32, 36, 42, 47, 49, 50, 54, 57, 71, 88, 89, 92-94, 96, 97, 101, 106, 111, 115

D
Discrimination, 19, 38, 51, 58, 62, 72, 114
Diversity, xiv, 1-3, 7, 9, 10, 12, 16, 18, 21, 29, 49, 51, 52, 55, 63, 65, 67, 85, 87, 96, 97, 99, 100, 110, 112-114, 120

E
Empowerment, 42, 91
Ethnicity, 3, 5, 15, 69
Ethnocentrism, 15, 16, 48, 58

H
Human needs, 5, 13, 25, 27, 31, 47, 69

I
International Declaration of Human Rights, 5, 31
Interpersonal interactions, 96

J
Journaling, 34, 72
Justice, 2, 38, 39, 41, 42, 53, 82

L
Language, 3, 6-8, 13, 18, 19, 27, 46, 48-50, 54, 55, 57, 87, 88, 93-96, 105, 107
Listening, 1, 46, 63, 71, 99, 101, 114, 118

M
Mission, xii, xiv, 2, 4, 8, 20, 23, 30, 31, 33, 34, 36, 37, 41, 56, 81, 82, 90, 107, 117, 118
Multicultural, 5, 6, 8, 16, 18, 45, 62, 85, 90, 94, 99-101, 110, 112, 113, 115, 119, 120

P
Pedagogy, 8, 30, 32, 33, 85, 91, 92, 114, 119, 120
Power, 12, 33, 41, 53, 105, 106, 115, 119
Powerlessness, 20, 106
Prejudice, 38, 57, 58, 60, 62, 72

R
Racism, 19, 5
Reflection, xiv, 2, 6, 7, 14, 18, 21, 31, 32, 34, 35, 37, 40-43, 50, 54, 58, 59, 66, 68, 90, 96-98, 109-112, 119
Reflective practitioner, 31,33
  Relationships, 2, 12, 19, 33, 38, 41, 44, 50, 71, 76, 96, 103, 104
Responsive pedagogy, 8, 85-87, 97-101, 120

S
Social analysis, 7, 75-77
Spiritual dimensions, xiv, 6, 30, 32, 33, 37, 41, 45, 71, 83, 112
Spirituality, xi, xii, xiv, 5, 6, 8, 23, 24, 28, 29, 33, 37, 41, 44, 83, 85, 90, 110, 111, 113
Stereotype, xii, 7, 52, 59-62, 64

V
Violence, 8, 13, 15, 27, 50, 53, 64, 103-105, 114

Studies in the Postmodern Theory of Education

General Editors
Joe L. Kincheloe & Shirley R. Steinberg

Counterpoints publishes the most compelling and imaginative books being written in education today. Grounded on the theoretical advances in criticalism, feminism, and postmodernism in the last two decades of the twentieth century, Counterpoints engages the meaning of these innovations in various forms of educational expression. Committed to the proposition that theoretical literature should be accessible to a variety of audiences, the series insists that its authors avoid esoteric and jargonistic languages that transform educational scholarship into an elite discourse for the initiated. Scholarly work matters only to the degree it affects consciousness and practice at multiple sites. Counterpoints' editorial policy is based on these principles and the ability of scholars to break new ground, to open new conversations, to go where educators have never gone before.

For additional information about this series or for the submission of manuscripts, please contact:
        Joe L. Kincheloe & Shirley R. Steinberg
        c/o Peter Lang Publishing, Inc.
        275 Seventh Avenue, 28th floor
        New York, New York 10001

To order other books in this series, please contact our Customer Service Department:
        (800) 770-LANG (within the U.S.)
        (212) 647-7706 (outside the U.S.)
        (212) 647-7707 FAX

Or browse online by series:
        www.peterlangusa.com